● ● ○ ○

A 2019 NSTA Best STEM Book

"Investigative journalist Redding does an admirable job of chronicling Larry and Sergey's amazing successes and will inspire young people to follow in their ingenious footsteps. It's more comprehensive than other books for young readers about Google's founders, with energetically written short chapters, interesting facts, graphics, and photos." —*Booklist,* starred review

"This readable and breezy history of the tech behemoth [is] an appealing and timely look at a universally relevant subject and a good fit for STEM-related reading lists." —*School Library Journal*

"Humorous accounts of Google's unpretentious beginnings as a student project, and its early years as a bare-bones startup in a friend's garage will intrigue teens who dream of growing their own projects into software and devices used by millions." —*VOYA*

● ● ○ ●

Also by ANNA CROWLEY REDDING

Elon Musk: A Mission to Save the World
(A 2020 NSTA Best STEM Book)

Black Hole Chasers:
The Amazing True Story of an Astronomical Breakthrough

Google It

It

A HISTORY *of* GOOGLE

• • •

ANNA CROWLEY REDDING

SQUARE
FISH
Feiwel and Friends
New York

SQUARE FISH

An imprint of Macmillan Publishing Group, LLC
120 Broadway, New York, NY 10271
fiercereads.com

Our books may be purchased in bulk for promotional, educational, or business
use. Please contact your local bookseller or the Macmillan Corporate and
Premium Sales Department at (800) 221-7945 ext. 5442 or by email at
MacmillanSpecialMarkets@macmillan.com.

The Library of Congress has cataloged the hardcover edition as follows:

Names: Redding, Anna Crowley, author.
Title: Google it : a history of Google / Anna Crowley Redding.
Description: First edition. | New York, NY : Feiwel and Friends, 2018 |
Includes bibliographical references. | Audience: Ages 12–18.
Identifiers: LCCN 2017041741 | ISBN 9781250148223 (hardcover)
Subjects: LCSH: Brin, Sergey, 1973—Juvenile literature. | Page, Larry, 1973—Juvenile
literature. | Computer programmers—United States—Biography—Juvenile literature. |
Telecommunications engineers—United States—Biography—Juvenile literature. |
Webmasters—United States—Biography—Juvenile literature. | Businesspeople—United
States—Biography—Juvenile literature. | Google (Firm)—Juvenile literature. | Google—
Juvenile literature. Classification: LCC QA76.2.A2 .R432018 | DDC 005.1092/2 [B]—dc23
LC record available at https://lccn.loc.gov/2017041741

Originally published in the United States by Feiwel and Friends
First Square Fish edition, 2021
Book designed by Raphael Geroni

Square Fish logo designed by Filomena Tuosto

ISBN 978-1-250-79210-5 (paperback)

10 9 8 7 6 5

AR: 6.5 / LEXILE: 870L

To Crowley and Quinn,
may you always shoot for the moon

CONTENTS

PART 1

Frenemies + Homework + Legos = Google?

CHAPTER 1

A Cold, Hard, Google-less World

N EED TO KNOW HOW many stacked pennies it would take to reach the moon? Want to know about the latest visual effects technology used to make *Star Wars*? Need to know if George Washington really had dentures made out of wood?

FYI:

- It would take a stack of 240 billion pennies to reach the moon!

- *Star Wars* special effects—Check out this cool link for a peek at how the latest computer graphics (CG) were used to pull off the stunning visuals. https://www.youtube.com/watch?v=obwG9k6x2us

- Was George Washington's wooden smile made from wooden teeth? NO. His *false* teeth were actually made of bone, ivory, and sometimes other humans' teeth.

Imagine you can't google the answers because—well, Google hasn't been invented yet.

You have two choices. You can sit there on your couch, swallow your curiosity like a bitter pill, and live with *not* knowing.

Or you can get your parents to drive you to the library. Fingers crossed, the answers you need are somewhere in the pages of a book that's somewhere on their bookshelves.

But wait a minute. What if your parents don't know how to get to the library? You'll have to consult a paper map.

WARNING! Unless you are an origami dynamo, once you unfold a map, it might never be refolded correctly. Never. Don't even try.

Still can't find it?

It may come down to this: You have to use a paper phone book to look up the library's phone number. Then, pick up your home phone (the kind that's wired to a wall), wait for a real, live human being to answer, and then *ask* for directions. Yikes!

It's hard to believe, but that was life without Google. Getting information was difficult and took a lot of work.

Horrified? The two guys who thought up Google were just as freaked out as you are. This was the world they grew up in, back in the 1970s and 1980s. And even as kids, Google co-founders Larry Page and Sergey Brin knew they wanted to change the world.

When Larry and Sergey were born in 1973, technology was in a very different place than it is today. In most homes, telephones were attached to walls and could only be used to make phone calls. No texts, no news, no maps—just phone calls. Hope was coming. That year, the first-ever cell phone call was made. But these cell phones were huge, like talking into a brick. Plus, the battery life was around twenty minutes. And then there was the price tag: $3,995! In today's dollars? That would set you back more than $22,000.

Oh, and about your TV. If you needed to change the channel, you had to get up and physically turn a dial on your TV set, unless you were one of the lucky ones who had a pricey remote control!

Computers had been something used mostly by scientists, engineers, and mathematicians in research and academic settings. They were physically huge and could take up an entire desk or even a whole room. But *this* last thing was about to change—just in time to inspire Larry's and Sergey's love of technology.

But it wouldn't be easy. Larry and Sergey were born on opposites sides of the planet. And when their paths finally crossed, they didn't even like each other.

It's a wonder Google ever happened at all.

● ● ●

Frenemies: Fight@1stSight

WHEN LARRY AND SERGEY MET DURING THE summer of 1995, they *should* have been the best of friends. After all, they both loved computers, math, engineering, science, and technology. They had both attended Montessori schools and grown up in families steeped in STEM. That's a lot in common.

BFFs at first sight, right? Nope. Not even close.

When they met for the very first time, Larry and Sergey couldn't stand each other! Twenty-two-year-old Larry was supposed to be enjoying a welcome tour of San Francisco for new students checking out nearby Stanford University. Already accepted to Stanford, Larry was giving the university a thorough look-see before deciding if he wanted to study there—though secretly he couldn't believe Stanford wanted him!

Spanish colonists founded San Francisco in 1776. The Gold Rush of 1849 made San Francisco the largest city on the West Coast. Today, the San Francisco Bay Area is home to 8.7 million people, making it the fifth-largest metro area in America.

Enter twenty-one-year-old Sergey. He was the tour guide. Who better to lead the tour? As a second-year graduate student, Sergey was known for zipping around Stanford's hallways on Rollerblades. He was not only fun, he was smart, too. Sergey had already aced his required courses and now devoted a serious chunk of time to advanced swimming, trapeze lessons, and Ultimate Frisbee. (Oh! And some elective courses. He did fit *some* study into his free time.)

But as Larry and Sergey trudged up one hill and down another, this duo filled the streets of San Francisco with their bickering banter. They argued about anything and everything . . . needling, poking, prodding, questioning, interrupting, and talking down to each other. Their first meeting was a disaster.

The only thing the two agreed on was their opinion of the other. In a word? *Obnoxious*.

Aerial view of Stanford University. (Photo by Jrissman.)

The sprawling 8,000-acre Stanford University campus was designed by Frederick Law Olmsted (designer of New York City's famous Central Park). Sitting in the heart of Silicon Valley, Stanford has long been an incubator for creativity and innovation. Companies including Hewlett-Packard, Yahoo!, Cisco, Intuit, and SunMicrosystems can trace their origins to Stanford.

But the same chemistry that sparked the nonstop squabbling also acted like a magnet. By the time school started in the fall of 1995, Larry and Sergey had discovered that they actually had a lot in common, from their science-filled childhoods to their passion for technology and engineering, not to mention their undeniable knack for spirited debate. Both Larry and Sergey were confident in exploring new ideas and taking risks. They were also both obsessed with efficiency and improving the way things worked.

And in just a few months, they would team up on a school assignment that would change their lives—and ours, too.

● ● ● ●

SERGEY BRIN

NAME: Sergey Mikhaylovich Brin

DATE OF BIRTH: August 21, 1973

PLACE: Moscow, Russia

FIRST COMPUTER: Age 9, Commodore 64

Commodore 64. (Photo by Evan Amos.)

Sure, by today's standards, the Commodore 64 isn't much to look at, but this remains one of the most popular computers ever sold. Because of the quality of the audio and graphics, it was great for gaming. The Commodore 64 sold for $595 in 1982.

FAMILY: Sergey Brin was born into a family of intellectuals. His great-grandmother? A microbiologist. His grandfather? A math professor. Both of his parents were brilliant mathematicians.

They were also very brave. Faced with anti-Semitism and discrimination in their home country of Russia, Sergey's parents made the difficult choice to leave everything behind and start a new life in America. Sergey was only six years old.

Immigrating to the United States during the 1970s was no simple matter. Like many immigrants, the Brin family had to leave most of their belongings behind. But an American-based agency devoted to immigrants helped Sergey's family. The Hebrew Immigrant Aid Society helped the Brins navigate the paperwork and apply for visas, and even bought tickets to the US for the family. In 2009, thirty years after Sergey and his family arrived in the United States, Sergey gave $1 million to the agency that helped his family escape Russia and resettle in Maryland. In 2017, when US President Donald Trump announced an immigration order banning travel to the United States from several Muslim-majority countries, Sergey joined the crowd of protesters at San Francisco's airport, saying, "I am here because I am a refugee."[1]

Settling into a small home in Baltimore, Maryland, Sergey's father became a mathematics professor at the University of Maryland, and Sergey's mom became a research scientist for NASA at the Goddard Space Flight Center—something that would never have been possible for Jews in Russia.

SCHOOLING: At his Montessori school, Sergey immersed himself in puzzles, math, and science projects; by middle school, his teachers had realized he was a genuine math prodigy.

Sergey sailed through high school, graduating early while also accumulating a year of college credit. This allowed him to graduate from the University of Maryland at only nineteen and become one of the youngest students ever admitted to Stanford's PhD program.

COULDA-WOULDA-SHOULDA ALERT! MIT rejected Sergey's grad school application. The school probably wishes it could get a do-over.

BOOKSHELF: No one captured Sergey's attention quite like Richard P. Feynman, Nobel Prize winner in Physics. During Sergey's childhood, Feynman published several books, including: *"Surely You're Joking, Mr. Feynman!": Adventures of a Curious Character* (1985) and *"What Do You Care What Other People Think?": Further Adventures of a Curious Character* (1988).

RICHARD P. FEYNMAN (1918–1988) was a world-famous theoretical physicist and a pioneer in quantum computing and nanotechnology.

As a child, he was raised to ask questions and challenge the status quo. By the time he was eleven, Feynman had spent hours taking apart radios and tinkering in his own makeshift laboratory. He even built a burglar alarm for his bedroom!

Brilliant by any standard, Feynman also experienced anti-Semitism. Even though he'd mastered a host of advanced mathematics, Columbia University denied his application. The reason? The school only allowed a certain number of Jews into their program and had already met that quota. Feynman attended MIT instead.

In the 1940s, during World War II, Feynman worked at the supersecretive Los Alamos National Laboratory, collaborating on the most top-secret project of the day—the atomic bomb. Serious business, to be sure.

Like Sergey, Feynman was not only smart, but also fun . . . and enjoyed picking locks and playing pranks.

Feynman's contributions to physics, nanotechnology, and quantum computing make him one of the greatest physicists in American history.

Larry Page (left) and Sergey Brin. (Photo by Randi Lynn Beach.)

LARRY PAGE

NAME: Lawrence "Larry" Page

DATE OF BIRTH: March 26, 1973

PLACE: Lansing, Michigan

FIRST COMPUTER: Age 6, Exidy Sorcerer

Exidy Sorcerer. (Photo by Wolfgang Stief.)

The Exidy Sorcerer was made by a video/arcade game company, Exidy. The Sorcerer was faster than its competitors and offered better graphics, which improved gaming. It was also the first plug-in-and-go home computer, which meant you could take it out of the box, plug it in, and start using it. Prior to this, setting up and using computers required technical know-how that the average person just didn't have.

And a SHOUT-OUT to NO SHOUTING . . . one of the key selling points for this computer was that it offered both upper- and *lower*case letters for typing. Phew! Pipe down, everybody.

FAMILY: Larry Page was born into a house where life revolved around technology. Larry's father was a computer science and artificial intelligence professor at Michigan State University. Talk about a pioneer! His mother had a master's degree in computer science and worked as a database consultant.

SCHOOLING: Larry also attended a Montessori school. "I think I was the first kid in my elementary school to turn in a word-processed document," Larry recalled in an interview. (In the 1970s and 1980s, most homework assignments and even research papers were still handwritten.) Larry graduated from the University of Michigan. He majored in both computer science and business.

YIKES ALERT! MIT also rejected Larry's grad school application. Double whammy!

INSPIRATION: At twelve years old, Larry read about an inventor named Nikola Tesla. As he leafed through the pages of Tesla's biography, Larry realized he wanted to be an inventor, too.

But Larry also quickly identified a tragic flaw in Tesla's story, which he saw as a cautionary tale. Even though Tesla was an amazing inventor, he never found fame or fortune through his work while he was alive.

"I realized I wanted to invent things, but I also wanted to change the world," Larry said. "I wanted to get them out there, get them into people's hands so they can use them."[2]

NIKOLA TESLA (1856–1943) was an extraordinary inventor, leading the way at the dawn of electricity. Filing more than seven hundred patents, Tesla invented the Tesla coil, which is still used in radio technology today. He also experimented with X-rays and radio waves, and laid the foundation for wireless technology.

But Larry Page was right. Tesla was never as successful, as well-known, or as celebrated as his nemesis: Thomas Edison. Sometimes Tesla even had to dig ditches just to support himself. He died in New York City in 1943, poor and suffering from mental illness.

BOOKSHELF: When Larry Page read *The Design of Everyday Things* by Donald A. Norman (1988), he became inspired by Norman's main premise: The user is always right.

CHAPTER 2

. . . .

Homework

THERE'S HOMEWORK

and then there's **HOMEWORK**. There's the kind you knock off in five minutes and the kind that determines your whole entire life. As graduate students at Stanford, Larry Page and Sergey Brin faced the most epic homework assignment of all: the doctoral thesis.

It's like getting married—to your homework. First, you propose your carefully chosen topic to your professors. With their approval, you dive into the deep end of research, spending hours, days, weeks, months—however long it takes to break new ground, discover something, or deepen humanity's understanding of your topic. And if that's not enough pressure, the last step is to present your research to a panel of professors. Professors who are allowed to ask you questions about your work—even challenge you—and you have to defend what you've learned!

Larry knew he needed to find just the right topic for his doctoral thesis. And he quickly turned his attention to the World Wide Web. In 1995, the web was only six years old—just a baby. Back then, in the ancient times of the internet, there were only about ten million web pages. And each page generally took thirty seconds to load—an eternity.

Today the web is made up of 4.73 billion web pages (and counting).

LINGO ALERT! The web and the internet are not the same thing. The internet is a giant network of computers, connected by cables and wireless signals. This *network* of networks allows computers to exchange information. The web is all of the content—documents, files, folders, web pages, and other resources—available via the internet, and is connected through links.

Still, when Larry looked at the web, he didn't just see a bunch of clunky, primitive web pages. He saw a mathematical graph. Each web page was a point on the graph. And just like the dots on a graph are connected by lines, the websites were connected with links.

Now came the questions. Were these links important? What could links tell us about a single page on the internet? Larry wanted to know more.

That's when he noticed something interesting: It was easy to look at a web page and see how many *outgoing* links it had to other sites. They were right there on the page in hypertext, ready to be clicked. But what Larry wanted to know was how many other sites linked back to a particular page? How many *incoming* links referred to a page? In 1995, nobody knew.

Hypertext is interactive text that leads you to another document, aka a web page. Oftentimes it's highlighted in another color. You can simply move your pointer to the hypertext and click to travel to the linked document, or web page, or information.

Larry explained it to a reporter like this: "The early versions of hypertext had a tragic flaw: You couldn't follow links in the other direction."[3] Larry wanted to reverse that.

● ●   ●

Backlinks

W HEN YOU RUN FOR CLASS PRESIDENT, YOU'RE not elected based on the number of leaders *you* think are brilliant. Instead, you are elected by the number of people who vote for you. Put another way, your popularity isn't measured by how many people *you* like; it's by how many people like *you*.

Studying the structure of the internet, Larry discovered a similar truth. It's not how many sites *you* link to that matters. What matters is how many sites link to *your* page. The more sites that link to you, the more relevant, substantial, and credible your site is. Each time a web page links to you, it's like a vote of confidence. The more votes a page receives, the more credible and important it must be.

This idea reminded Larry of something that was talked about a lot in his house when he was growing up: citation.

Suppose you are a scientist, brilliantly plugging away at research on climate change. You discover new evidence and prove new theories about how humans are changing the climate. You publish these discoveries in a scientific journal. Two things can happen. Your work can be ignored. Or it can be of such importance that scientists around the globe start talking about it. Building on your work, other scientists take your research to the next level with more investigations, experiments, and evidence. And when they publish their conclusions, they mention you. They *cite* your paper, your research, your contribution. Each mention is called a citation. And if hundreds and even thousands of scientists cite your work? It says the quality and credibility of your work is important. The more your work is cited, the more its importance grows.

Larry wondered if he could analyze the backlinks to figure out the credibility of a web page just as citation validated research. It was a big idea. And pulling it off would be complicated.

To accomplish this goal, Larry needed to search the World Wide Web, survey web pages, count their backlinks, and rank those results. This would require a sophisticated mathematical algorithm.

A mathematical algorithm is a specific set of steps that are followed in order to solve a math problem or to perform and complete a computer process. Another way to think about an algorithm is to look at it like a recipe for baking. Step-by-step instructions are followed to achieve a specific goal.

And he knew just the right mathematical mind for the job: Sergey Brin. It turned out that Sergey was still searching for his thesis topic, too. He found Larry's idea fascinating "because it tackled the web, which represents human knowledge," Sergey recalled to a reporter, "and because I liked Larry."[4]

But it wouldn't be easy. After all, they were planning to count and analyze all the links for the *entire* web, all ten million pages. They would need to deploy a crawler, harvest the links, store them, and then start analyzing their value. This meant downloading the World Wide Web—the whole thing.

Web crawlers have a couple of other cool names: spiders and internet bots! A crawler is nothing more than a program that visits web pages and reads them. Each crawler (or bot) is on the hunt for specific information. Once found, the spider then creates a database or index of what it has discovered, making the information easier to access.

The bandwidth required for such a task would need to be enormous, far beyond that of a typical Stanford student project.

This was a way bigger deal. Not to mention, they were going to move around a lot of data and would need a server that could store and handle that much information.

A server is a computer with a specific job or set of tasks that it performs. There are many different kinds of servers. Some store files or manage network traffic or deliver web pages, for example. The server's software determines what its job is.

Bandwidth is a measurement of how fast a computer can send data. It's often measured in bits per second. The smallest unit of data in a computer is known as a binary digit, or *bit* for short. A bit is either a *1* or a *0*. When you talk about bits per second, you are talking about how fast these smallest pieces of data are transmitted or received in one second.

Back in 1995, people had modems that connected to the internet over phone lines. The maximum speed was 0.056 megabits per second (Mbps). Today, most people in America connect to the internet with speeds of at least 20 Mbps. That means today we can download photographs in an instant. But back then, even downloading one low-quality image could take several minutes.

• • • •

Beg, Borrow, Stalk

WHAT DO YOU DO WHEN YOU NEED A TON OF computer equipment but don't have a ton of money? That was the problem Larry and Sergey faced. Sitting in their grad school office, also known as Gates 360 (yes, it's named after *that* Gates, Bill Gates of Microsoft), Larry and Sergey quickly concocted a stealthy plan.

Lurking around the loading dock of Stanford University's computer science building, Larry and Sergey spied on computer deliveries. They found out exactly how many computers were delivered and who was getting them.

Then they made their pitch!

Hello.

We noticed you received a shipment of twenty computers this morning.

Surely you could make do with nineteen?

And so they went, door to door, delivery by delivery, begging for parts and borrowing computers. Spending what little money they had and snatching up any "unclaimed" deliveries (some call it stealing, others call it borrowing—indefinitely), Larry and Sergey collected the necessary odds and ends.

Not only were computers really expensive back then, they were heavy, too. Which made moving them around kind of hard. So Larry and Sergey actually purchased a big cart to lug the crates of "found" and "borrowed" computers back to their office.

Luckily, they shared that space with an equally quirky cast of characters.

Now that they had a host of computer components, electronics, and disks, it was time to piece it all together.

And what better tool for that task than . . . LEGOS! Or rather the least expensive alternative they could find. As poor college students, Larry and Sergey decided that they couldn't afford real Legos.

As a student at the University of Michigan, Larry nailed a school assignment by building an inkjet printer out of Legos! Little did he know that those brick-building skills were about to play a big part in accomplishing his goal of changing the world.

Building blocks strewn across Larry's desk, the pair began to snap the plastic bricks together. Soon multicolored towers emerged from the mess. Placing the hard disks into the tower, their homemade server was complete. Some corners were even held together with tape.

Google's first server storage rack (made from Lego Duplo blocks after the original knockoff brand collapsed). (Photo by Steve Jurvetson.)

Google's original server was made up of ten 4 gigabyte (GB) drives, a total of 40 GB. In 1996, 4 GB disks were the largest disks available. Today, you can buy a hard drive that fits in the palm of your hand and holds 16 terabytes of data (which is about 16,000 GB).

You can see the original server for yourself. It's on display at Stanford University's Engineering Center.

Today, it's estimated that Google has about one million servers in use!

Now came the moment of truth. Sergey and Larry plugged their creation into Stanford's computer network and began to download the web.

It worked. And their experiment was crawling the web and downloading it.

"Google" was born.

Actually, um . . . make that . . . BackRub. That's right. BackRub. Yes, when Larry and Sergey considered a name for their soon-to-be-life-changing idea, they came up with BackRub.

And technically, they had just achieved the first step in the process: crawling and downloading the web. But BackRub was simply a web crawler, an amazing one, but still . . . Now Larry and Sergey had the herculean task of making mathematical sense of all this data.

● ● ● ●

GATES 360 OFFICE TOUR

MEET THE OFFICE MATES: SEAN ANDERSON WAS A STUDENT SO INTENSE about his studies that the lost time in his apartment would not do. He started working *and* sleeping in the office. He also filled the office with plants, then programmed his computer to water them.

Tamara Munzner was the only woman in the group. To get her work done, she wore headphones to drown out Larry and Sergey's still-infamous "debates." An energetic Lucas Pereira and a quiet Ben Zhu rounded out the office mates.

As PhD students, Larry and Sergey also had two paid research assistants: Scott Hassan and Alan Steremberg. Both Scott and Alan were Stanford students, looking to earn a little money and work on a cool project. When Alan wasn't helping Larry and Sergey, he was toying with his own project, Weather Underground. It would become one of the most popular weather-forecasting sites because of accuracy and level of detail. And Alan became the president of Weather Underground.

Scott Hassan got the research assistant job after meeting Sergey at an Ultimate Frisbee game at Stanford. He was a talented programmer and equally gifted at pulling pranks. Hassan went on to become a pioneer in robotics and today is developing a robot that marries a rolling body with a flat-screen TV for a head. Instead of talking to a robot, you can have a *live* video chat with the robot's owner, kind of like you do on a FaceTime call. Maybe, in the future, instead of going to class, you can just send your robot! Hassan's innovation is called the Beam.

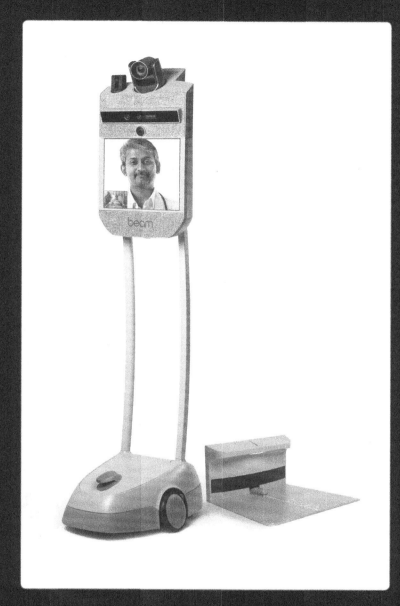

A Beam Pro robot. (Photo © Suitable Technologies.)

CHAPTER 3

The Long-Lost Nightmare: Search Before Google

T

ODAY, IF YOU TYPE "Why is William Shakespeare important?" into Google, you'll end up with hundreds of thousands of results in only 0.63 seconds. And all those results will be ranked by importance. No big deal, right?

Wrong!

Prepare yourself. This trip in the time machine is going to be bumpy.

Before Google, humans lived in a world where search results were meaningless. You logged onto a search engine. You typed in a basic keyword like "Shakespeare" because the search engine couldn't handle conversational text. You might be wondering, *Where was Shakespeare born?* But all you typed in was William's last name.

> Conversational text is a phrase or sentence that sounds the same way you might speak it. It's an informal and natural expression of your thoughts or questions.

You hit return and waited as pages and pages of results loaded, in no particular order. In fact, the very thing you were looking for might be found in the very last result—or somewhere in the middle. Even worse? An hour into searching, you were probably hit with a roar-worthy realization: You needed to type in a different keyword (and do it all over again). You try to scream, but you can't even muster a whisper.

The problem? Internet searches were based on keywords. So if you were looking for information about horses, web searches would give you every site that mentioned the word *horse*. And you would have to sit there and load each result, searching for the information you needed.

It was as if you walked into a library and asked for information on horses. And the librarian took every book, magazine, and brochure that so much as mentioned the word. Then he dumped them in random, mixed-up piles for you to riffle through until you found what you were looking for. That was search before Google, a memory few people dare to talk about. What we needed was a way to organize this information.

PageRank

SERGEY BRIN'S MATH BRAIN WAS THE PERFECT noggin to noodle over an algorithm that would analyze the links and rank web pages. It was like a recipe for a signature dish. And Larry and Sergey named this special sauce PageRank.

Notice anything familiar about the word *PageRank*? You guessed it! Larry and Sergey named it after Larry, using his last name, Page.

Imagine you published a web page gushing over *The Force Awakens* (and rightfully so). How could an algorithm know the difference between your site and that of, say, StarWars.com? Which site is more relevant? More credible? More important to the topic?

The answer is in the backlinks. Chances are, as true as your devotion must be, you do not have as many people linking to your fan site as StarWars.com does. After all, StarWars.com offers inside scoops, games, videos, behind-the-scenes footage, sneak peeks, etc. Meanwhile, your fan site might have one post on how that movie impressed you.

PageRank can determine which site is more important based on the number of incoming links. And here's a brain bender: It's not just how many links are pointing to your site, it's how important those referring sites are . . . which is determined by the number of incoming links *they* have.

Then, once a particular page had a PageRank score, Sergey also figured out a way to analyze factors like keywords, capitalization, font size, the distance between words on a page, and more. These clues are called signals. Analyzing all these signals helped Sergey develop an algorithm that painted a pretty clear picture of a web page's relevance.

As Larry told an interviewer, "We convert the entire web into a big equation with several hundred million variables, which are the PageRanks of all the web pages, and billions of terms, which are the links."[5] In other words, the web was just a giant, complicated math problem. One that Larry and Sergey solved.

When inventors create something new, they file a patent for their invention. This paperwork protects the invention so others can't copy it. Since PageRank was created by Stanford grad students on campus, Stanford University owns the patent for PageRank. Stanford licensed this patent exclusively to Google in exchange for stock in the company. When the school sold these 1.8 million shares in Google in 2005, it made $336 million. Not bad! (I guess that makes up for the missing computers.) Check out the patent here: https://www.google.com/patents/US6285999.

In 1996, as Larry and Sergey deployed BackRub to crawl the web and create an index of the links, they then unleashed PageRank to organize and rank all that web data. While analyzing the results, they realized their project was a lot like—well, *a lot like* a search engine, only with accurate results. Eureka! They compared those query results with those of the most popular search engines of the day. No question about it. PageRank's results were the best by a long shot.

Like any web surfer worth their weight in ones and zeroes, Larry first used BackRub to search . . . his own name.

Larry and Sergey realized that they had just accidentally revolutionized web search.

BackRub is a "web crawler" which is designed to traverse the web.

Currently we are developing techniques to improve web search engines. We will make various services available as soon as possible.

We have a demo that searches the titles of over 16 million urls: BackRub title search demo

BackRub search with comparison (type in top box, ignore cgi-bin error) New systems will be coming soon.
Some documentation from a talk about the system is here.

BackRub is a research project of the Digital Library Project in the Computer Science Department at Stanford University.

Some Rough Statistics (from August 29th, 1996)
Total indexable HTML urls: 75.2306 Million
Total content downloaded: 207.022 gigabytes
Total indexable HTML pages downloaded: 30.6255 Million
Total indexable HTML pages which have not been attempted yet: 30.6822 Million
Total robots.txt excluded: 0.224249 Million
Total socket or connection errors: 1.31841 Million

BackRub is written in Java and Python and runs on several Sun Ultras and Intel Pentiums running Linux. The primary database is kept on an Sun Ultra II with 28GB of disk. Scott Hassan and Alan Steremberg have provided a great deal of very talented implementation help. Sergey Brin has also been very involved and deserves many thanks.

Before emailing, please read the FAQ. Thanks.

-Larry Page page@cs.stanford.edu

Screenshot of the original BackRub home page via Internet Archive WayBack Machine.

• ∘ ⋮ ●

Liftoff

Buzz about BackRub whipped around campus like a wildfire. Students in particular were very excited: It's not every day you get hours of your life back. The days of sifting through meaningless search results were over. Minds were blown. Jaws dropped.

For the first time, you could search the web and quickly find useful information—even the very thing you were looking for!

It wasn't long before ten thousand people were using Back-Rub every day.

The demand for BackRub boomed. And it wasn't the only thing booming.

The web was growing at a crazy rate, tripling in size from 1996 to 1997.

That meant Larry and Sergey needed ever more computers and disk storage to crawl the ever-expanding web and to store an ever-increasing amount of links.

Racing to keep up with the demand, they added computers, miscellaneous parts, and racks—their bulging DIY server quickly consumed their corner of the office. Larry's dorm room was next. They filled it with servers. Sergey sacrificed his room, too. Now it was BackRub's business office.

But as Larry and Sergey's server network grew, their electricity supply did not. They needed access to the circuit breaker, which was located in the *locked* basement. But the lack of a key (or permission) did not stymie them for long. Sergey turned to one of his favorite books for help: *MIT Guide to Lock Picking*. You can guess what happened next. They let themselves into the basement and gave their bulging computer system a power boost.

Getting to the basement also solved another problem: the issue of bandwidth. With one flip of a toggle switch, BackRub could have access to Stanford's full bandwidth of 45 Mbps instead of the mere 10 Mbps allotted to their building. Switch re-toggled, they had more than quadrupled their bandwidth.

But as much power as they added to the project, they always needed more. Their innovative homework experiment regularly brought down the school's internet connection. They used up over half of Stanford's bandwidth. And BackRub wasn't just consuming tons of electricity, server space, and internet connection; it also consumed Larry and Sergey's every waking hour.

● ● ●

LET ME GIVE YOU A LITTLE ADVICE . . .

WHEN LARRY AND SERGEY JOINED STANFORD'S GRADUATE PROGRAM, THEY were each assigned an advisor, or a professor who would help shepherd them through their journey to a PhD. It's an important relationship: a person to bounce ideas off, help you solve problems, get ideas for new directions or managing research, approve your thesis topic, and any number of things (good, bad, and difficult) that come up.

Larry was assigned Terry Winograd, a pioneer in human-computer interaction (HCI). Winograd was no stranger to Larry. No, years earlier when Larry was a little boy, his dad spent a sabbatical at Stanford—with Larry in tow. Some faculty still remembered that curious seven-year-old from long ago. And Larry remembered Terry Winograd.

Winograd loved that Larry had big ideas and the belief that he could make them reality. When Larry talked about his interest in the emerging World Wide Web, Winograd encouraged him to pursue his thesis on that topic.

In a 1996 e-mail between Larry and his advisor, Larry asked for help in getting more disk space. Downloading the web was expensive because it took up so much disk space. Larry wrote to Winograd that retail prices for disk space was a thousand dollars for 4 GB. He needed 8 GB, he thought. He would actually need a heck of a lot more than that—Google's first server used 40 GB!

Winograd also ran interference for early complaints. Sites could tell that BackRub was requesting their web pages, and some of the people running those sites didn't understand why and also didn't appreciate it.

Sergey's advisor was the chair of the Computer Science Department, Hector Garcia-Molina, who was immediately struck by Sergey's brilliance. Sergey also spent a great deal of time getting advice from

Stanford professor Rajeev Motwani. While Motwani was not an official advisor, Sergey came to him regularly with technical questions.

"When my interest turned to data mining, Rajeev helped coordinate a regular meeting group on the subject," Sergey wrote years later in a blog post. "Even though I was just one of hundreds of graduate students in the department, he always made the time and effort to help. Later, when Larry and I began to work together on the research that would lead to Google, Rajeev was there to support us and guide us through challenges, both technical and organizational."[6]

After Sergey left Stanford, he and Motwani continued to stay in close contact. And when Motwani unexpectedly passed away in 2009, Google endowed a $2.5 million Stanford professorship in his memory.

These advisors played key roles in shaping Larry's and Sergey's education, research, and innovation. Now Larry and Sergey would need their help to navigate some very tough decisions.

CHAPTER 4

· · · · · · ·

#Spelling

I N 1 9 9 7 , T H E W O R L D was saved from a terrible fate: *Back-Rubbing* everything for all of eternity!

Hey, can you BackRub movie times for Friday night?

Hey, BackRub Barack Obama.

Now, students, get out your computers and BackRub the first Thanksgiving.

Wow. Let's have a moment of gratitude for the fact that Larry and Sergey faced the ugly truth: *BackRub* was a terrible name. Larry realized BackRub simply did not have the snap or pizzazz of other web companies like Yahoo! or Excite. It wasn't catchy. It wasn't fresh. It wasn't cutting-edge. Also it would have been kind of creepy as a verb.

Larry and Sergey turned to their fellow graduate students and office mates for help.

Brainstorming sessions produced lots of ideas. But when their grad school buddy Sean Anderson floated the term *Googolplex*, heads turned.

Larry instantly thought it should be shortened to Googol. And, no, I didn't spell that wrong.

Googol is the number 1 followed by 100 zeroes or 10 to the 100th power. The number googol got its name from a nine-year-old boy, Milton Sirotta. Milton's uncle was an accomplished mathematician and asked Milton what they should call such a large number. Milton thought googol was perfect in all its silliness.

Googol is such a huge number that Larry and Sergey felt it zeroed in on PageRank's enormous possibilities better than any word they could think of. After all, the bigger the web became, the greater the search results. Every additional link added to the web was more data to mine, more citations. Indeed—an ever-clearer picture of any one page's relevance.

Just like you mine rock for new materials, like diamonds, you can mine a large database for the sole purpose of finding new information. Even better? Find information that's never been discovered. That's the diamond of data mining. And in this case, the data was links; the diamond was the information backlinks offered about any site's importance or credibility.

Larry and Sergey thought *Googol* had the zip, jazz, and snap that *BackRub* lacked. Plus, they thought, it was easy to type and even easier to remember. So, on September 15, 1997, Larry and Sergey quickly registered the domain name. Problem solved!

Except for one minor issue . . . Okay, major issue.

They had misspelled the word! G-O-O-G-L-E.

Office mate Tamara Munzner pointed out the mistake the next day. Ouch!

But let's not judge them too harshly! Apparently, we can't spell, either. In 2000, Britney Spears topped the pop charts with her hit "Oops!... I Did It Again." People began searching "Britney Spears" on Google. The results? Dozens upon dozens of misspellings of her name. Oops! That data—the long list of misspellings—got Google's attention.

"We noticed a lot of people were interested in Britney Spears, but not all of them could spell," said Google's first employee, Craig Silverstein.[7] That realization led Google to expand. Not only would Google provide search results, they would begin offering spelling correction, too.

Staring at *Google* scrawled across a whiteboard, Larry and Sergey realized they actually liked Googol's new spelling more.

Their project now had a snappy name and lots of users. Plus—remembering that mother of all homework assignments— technically they had expanded humanity's understanding of their topic.

In terms of homework, they were killing it. But a large question remained. Had Google crossed the threshold from homework to business? Should Google become a company? Could it become a bona fide moneymaker? This question wasn't unheard of among Stanford's graduate students. The campus produced business after business after business.

But Google's growth and wild popularity demanded an answer—and fast.

Larry and Sergey weren't sure what to do. The pair were worried that if Google was indeed a business, they'd have to drop out of school to run it.

And dropping out of school to see this idea through . . . wasn't their first choice. Not by a long shot.

• · •

Grad School Dropouts

IMAGINE YOUR FAMILY TREE IS FILLED WITH professors, mathematicians, researchers, and scientists—people who value education more than anything. Would you want to call them up and announce you are dropping out of school?

No? Me, either.

But Larry and Sergey had to face the facts: Google was growing at quite a clip. It had outgrown its "homework" label. And it would quickly need a full-time staff to run it.

Something had to give—either school or Google. After seeking advice from advisors and mentors, Larry and Sergey came to a decision. They would sell Google and stay in school. As Stanford students, in the heart of Silicon Valley, they had access to the movers and shakers of the tech world. And everyone was talking about Google. Win-win, right?

Not exactly. As Larry and Sergey soon discovered, no one wanted to buy it.

In 1997, search company AltaVista was hot. And Larry believed that he could make AltaVista a ton of money if the company bought Google. He offered it to them for $1 million. But AltaVista didn't like buying technology from company outsiders. So they said no.

Today, AltaVista is out of business.

Wait! Hang on. Companies had a chance to buy Google for only a million bucks, a tiny fraction of what it is worth today? And they took a pass?

Yes. It was one of those awkward it's-not-you-it's-me-I'm-just-not-that-into-search conversations.

When Larry and Sergey approached popular web search engine Excite, negotiations progressed. Larry and Sergey wanted $1.6 million. The management team at Excite was struggling to put together an offer of even $350,000. The Excite team wasn't sure if they really wanted Google.

After Larry and Sergey talked it over, they finally sent Excite an e-mail, a final offer. Sergey remembers what happened next, word for word. "We fired off a note, a little e-mail," he later recounted to a captivated audience in an auditorium full of people. "You know, we don't really want to sell . . . but, for $1.6 million, you've got a deal."

Sergey laughed when he talked about what happened next. "A few minutes later we got a reply that said, 'That's a lot of dough, but okay, we'll do it!'" But ten minutes later, one of their graduate assistants, Scott Hassan, came running into the room, laughing. "He had a huge grin on his face because he had faked Excite's reply!"[8] Even though a real deal never came to be, Sergey and Larry still get a big kick out of that prank.

The big search engines of the day wanted to act more as a web hub or hangout for people. These busy "web portals" did have a search function, but they also offered news, e-mail, weather, horoscopes, and more. The head honchos of those companies believed if people logged on to your portal and stuck around, they would see banner ads—and banner ads would bring in money.

"We realized by talking to all the CEOs of search companies—which were really turning into portals—that commercially, no one was going to develop search engines. They said, 'Oh, we don't really care about our search engine.' And we realized there was a huge business opportunity and that nobody else was going to work on it."[9]
—Larry Page

Larry and Sergey, on the other hand, had figured out how to improve web search. And while that would make people's lives easier, it would also get them off the web portal faster, and away from the banner ads. Larry and Sergey believed in Google. But month after month, as rejection after rejection rolled in, Larry and Sergey's frustration grew.

With no buyers, Larry and Sergey realized what must be done. If they truly believed in Google, in organizing the web, and making information easy for anyone to find, the pair would have to start the company themselves.

And to do that—they had to make that awkward phone call home to tell their parents they were dropping out of school.

"We were definitely upset," Sergey's mom, Eugenia Brin, told a biographer. "We thought everybody in their right mind ought to get a PhD."[10]

Sergey's dad was equally clear on the hopes he had for his son. "I expected him to get his PhD. And become somebody, maybe a professor," said Michael Brin.[11]

For Larry, the decision to leave school was particularly poignant. There's no question that Larry's drive to develop BackRub, PageRank, and Google was entrepreneurial, academic, and innovative. But it was also a way to process his grief.

While Larry was at Stanford, his father died unexpectedly at age fifty-eight. Larry and his father had been close. They enjoyed a mutual love of debate, Grateful Dead concerts, and innovation. And finishing his degree was, in part, a way to honor his dad.

But as Sergey told one biographer, it was an academic advisor's perspective that made a huge difference. The advisor pointed out that if Google didn't work out, Larry and Sergey could always come back and finish their degree. In fact, school could wait, but Google could not. Its time was now.

This made sense to Larry, too. As he later explained in an interview, "If the company failed, too bad. We were doing something that mattered."[12]

Decision made, parents told, Larry and Sergey had one more hurdle to jump: money. The constant quest for more computers, parts, and storage had not been easy on their wallets. They had both maxed out their credit cards. Plus, Sergey estimated that every time the duo deployed a spider to crawl the web, it cost Stanford about twenty thousand dollars. As Google grew and the web grew, they—as always—needed more computers. They needed money, and fast.

That summer (1998), Google had about twenty-four million websites in its database. And the number was growing by the minute.

They needed an investor. But they had already failed to sell Google. How were they going to find someone who not only understood what they were doing but wanted to hand over some money to fund it?

Enter Andy Bechtolsheim. He was the vice president of Cisco Systems and had invested in other start-ups as an angel investor. One of Larry and Sergey's Stanford advisors had mentioned Google to Andy.

Andy Bechtolsheim. (Photo by David Paul Morris.)

Andy immediately asked for a demonstration. As soon as Andy saw what Google could do, he looked at Larry and Sergey and said, "Well, I don't want to waste time. I'm sure it'll help you guys if I just write a check."[13]

Just like that, Andy reached for his checkbook. In a matter of seconds, he handed over a check for a hundred thousand dollars! Larry and Sergey stared at it. The check was made out to Google Inc., a company that did not yet exist. They didn't even have a bank account.

An angel investor is a person who provides seed money to a start-up to get an idea or company up and running. In Larry and Sergey's case, once Andy signed on, others followed, including Jeff Bezos of Amazon.com.

As Andy drove away, Larry and Sergey looked at each other. Wow. It was time to celebrate. This was a major milestone. A huge accomplishment. They needed to mark the moment. They needed to eat something really good—but also cheap (remember, they couldn't cash that check yet). They knew just the place. And so, Larry and Sergey, founders of Google, headed straight for . . . Burger King! That's right, Burger King.

And then they headed back to campus, stuffed the check into a desk drawer, began filing the paperwork to incorporate, and took the leap!

On September 8, 1998, Google Inc. officially became a company. It was exciting but also risky. What if the company crashed and burned?

• • •

America's Most Misspelled Words

Top searched "how to spell" by state, 2017

1 to 5 letters ●
6 to 10 letters ●
11 to 19 letters ●
20+ letters ●

Google Trends

PNEUMONIA

SENSE

SURPRISE

QUOTE

PRIORITY

AVAILABLE

DISEASE

TOMO

BEAUTIFUL

TOMORROW

BANANA

SCHEDULE

PEO

Screenshot of "America's Most Misspelled Words by State" via Google Trends.

CHAPTER 5

Google World Headquarters

L ARRY AND SERGEY might not have graduated from Stanford, but their company sure did. Google was no longer just a school project. It was officially a business, which meant it was time for Larry and Sergey to put that hundred-thousand-dollar check in the bank, pack up their dorm rooms, and head for a bright, new, shiny office.

The two forked over $1,700 a month to their friend, and now landlord, Susan Wojcicki.

Welcome to Google World Headquarters—um, also known as Susan's garage. It wasn't fancy, but make no bones about it—there is something awfully handy about a garage door when you need fresh air fast.

Susan Wojcicki. (Photo © Google.)

Time magazine named the brilliant and accomplished Susan Wojcicki one of the most influential people of 2015. And it's no surprise. She was raised by a mother who focused on intelligence, independence, and questioning the status quo—rather than looks and "appropriate" behavior for girls. Questioning authority was a staple of the Wojcicki family diet.

A Harvard graduate, Susan also has a master's degree and MBA. Like Sergey and Larry, Susan thought she would have an academic career—until she fell in love with technology. A marketing whiz, Susan eventually threw caution to the wind in order to work for the start-up in her garage. And she hasn't looked back. Susan went on to become the CEO of YouTube, which is owned by Google.

Larry and Sergey quickly filled the space with their DIY servers on DIY desks (old doors laid on top of wooden sawhorses). Their rent also included two downstairs bedrooms. That's where you found the real gem of the deal: old, stained turquoise shag carpet.

Shag carpet is supposed to be a dense forest of loopy yarn that offers a luxurious plush feel when you tread upon its pet-able yarn. But that plush foot hug only ever happened on *new* shag carpet. As it ages, it clumps, it stains, it moistens, turning each barefoot step into a bit of a horror mystery. Heaven help you if you ever drop a staple in that shag—it's waiting for you, ready to strike and draw blood from your big toe when you least expect it.

Even with the yucky carpet, they felt they'd found the perfect place to start. Now a 24/7 operation, Larry and Sergey not only worked there but lived there, too. They worked hard, but quietly. The landlord lived in the rest of the house with her husband. And she was expecting her first baby.

Larry and Sergey quickly welcomed Google's first employee: Craig Silverstein, a friend and fellow student from Stanford. But when Larry and Sergey discovered Craig's old Porsche backfired every time it started, the Google co-founders made sure to push that Porsche quietly down the street before Craig cranked the engine!

Google World Headquarters, aka Susan's garage.
(Photo by Justin Sullivan/Getty Images.)

232 Santa Margarita Avenue, Menlo Park, California. Want to see it for yourself? Google bought it for a million bucks in 2006. It's become a techie tourist hot spot. Fair warning: You can't go inside. And the neighbors may not exactly love the steady stream of tour buses motoring by.

Meet Google's first employee: Craig Silverstein. Okay, technically, he was employee number three after Larry and Sergey. Craig would work for Google for more than ten years. In 2008, he left Google to oversee infrastructure at Khan Academy, a nonprofit devoted to offering free online education to anyone anywhere in the world.

Craig Silverstein. (Photo by Paul Sakuma.)

While Larry, Sergey, and Craig quietly worked away, the buzz about Google grew to a roar. Google found its way to the pages of one of the most important technology magazines: *PC Magazine*. It was an authoritative giant on all things computer and tech. And that December 1998, the magazine's editors named Google as one of the top 100 websites—with an "uncanny knack for returning extremely relevant results." The article went on to say, "There's much more to come at Google!"

Yes, there was much more to come from Google. That said, Google was *not* making any money. Not a dime. Not a nickel. Not a penny. But Larry and Sergey didn't let that stop them. They focused instead on fine-tuning their vision for Google. And that's when they began to realize Google was going to change the world. They believed the money would follow, even though they had not worked out exactly how that would happen or when. But they believed anyway.

On the outside of the garage, a handwritten sign read, GOOGLE WORLD HEADQUARTERS. Inside, even more important words came together to form Google's mission statement: "To organize the world's information and make it universally accessible and useful."

Yeah. Just that. Organize the world's information.

● ∙ ●

The Power of the (Almost) Blank Page

Our goal is to
design everything so it's
beautifully simple.[14]

—LARRY PAGE

GOOGLE'S SEARCH RESULTS WERE A REVOLUTION, a rebellion, a revolt. But the search results were only part of this new world order. Google's look was also a whole other frontier.

WARNING! You're gonna need eye drops and sunglasses for this trip in the time machine.

Help! The web is attacking my eyes!

Okay, before Google, search engines didn't actually attack your physical eyeballs. But visually? It was an all-out assault. We've already talked about how search sites wanted to be web portals; that meant, on a single page, there was a jungle of horoscopes, news, e-mail, entertainment news, shopping, and more. It was a barrage of information. Ack! Now add in the advertisements. Sprinkle them here and there. And don't forget the giant banner ad sprawled across the top of the page, flashing away to grab your attention.

eXcite
search   *reviews*   city.net   *live!*   *tours* NEW
people finder ——— maps ——— yellow pages ——— news

Excite DIRECT
"Turbo Search!"
Download
Excite Direct

Excite Search: twice the power of the competition.
What: [   ] *search*
Where: [World Wide Web   ▼]   [Help]
                                                [Advanced Search]

Take an
ExciteSeeing Tour

Excite on TV

INTEGRATED BROWSING, EMAIL,
NEWSGROUPS AND PAGE CREATION.   N NETSCAPE Now!

Excite Reviews: site reviews by the web's **best editorial team.**

○ Arts	○ Entertainment	○ Money	○ Regional
○ Business	○ Health	○ News & Reference	○ Science
○ Computing	○ Hobbies	○ Personal Pages	○ Shopping
○ Education	○ Life & Style	○ Politics & Law	○ Sports

AOL Members' Choice
N NETSCAPE Now!
Microsoft Internet Explorer e FREE!

Make your website
searchable. FREE!

Excite City.Net
Plan your weekend, your
travels.
Find-A-Destination
[   ]
[Take me there!]
Maps ○ Top Cities ○ Concierge

ExciteSeeing Tours
Choose from hundreds.

○ X-Files: The truth is out there!
○ Dr. Ruth's guide to safer sex
○ Windows 95 shareware and freeware
○ Celebrating Thanksgiving
○ Investing in high-tech stocks
○ New to the Net?

Excite Live!
Your news, your way.

○ Latest news	○ Stock quotes
○ Sports scores	○ TV listings
○ Local weather	○ Horoscopes
○ Movie reviews	○ Site reviews

Excite Reference
Just the facts, ma'am.

○ Yellow Pages	○ Maps
○ People Finder	○ Shareware
○ Email Lookup	○ Dictionary

eXcite
search   *reviews*   city.net   *live!*   *tours* NEW
people finder ——— maps ——— yellow pages ——— news

©1996 Excite Inc.
Feedback

Screenshot of Excite search page in October 1996
via Internet Archive WayBack Machine.

Just try to take it all in. Your eyes dart up and down, back and forth, focusing, blurring, getting lost. That visual jungle sucked every last drop of moisture out of your eyeballs. And after a few moments sitting there with your dry red eyes, you don't even remember what you logged on for!

The CEOs of these search engines thought this concept was brilliant. People were spending a lot of time on these web portals, clicking and clicking and clicking. And those CEOs were counting clicks all the way to the bank. More clicks meant more eyeballs to take in the ads. If you are clicking on stuff, you are spending time in the portal. Which means, even if you tried, you can't ignore the ads. You are getting the message. And advertisers were willing to pay for your attention.

It was a lot like binge-watching a really lame series. And about ten episodes in, someone walks into your room and says, "Why are you watching this lame show?" Jolted back to planet Earth, you wonder where you are, what your name is, and where you've been all day. It hits you all at once: I just wasted hours and I didn't even want to watch that garbage.

Only in this case, it wasn't a friend who walked into the room and woke you up; it was Google.

The page was white. No sections, no buttons, no horoscopes. It was nearly blank—except for the simple logo, *Google*, spelled out in blue, red, yellow, and green, and an economy of text. Simple. Clean.

Screenshot of Google.com in November 1999 via Internet Archive WayBack Machine.

When you need a supercool logo but money is in short supply, what do you do? Well, if you are Sergey, you certainly don't let lack-o-money stop you. You just design it yourself. Sergey used a free graphics program known as GIMP. Just because it was free didn't mean it was easy. But with some work, Sergey figured it out. Users loved the logo's simplicity. And even though Google's logo would eventually get a professional tweak, the signature simplicity would remain.

Google logo as of September 2017. (© Google)

It was better than eye drops.

It was a relief.

Google was easy on the eyes and easy to use.

Exactly as Larry and Sergey wanted. It all went back to their fundamental belief: The user is always right. And they knew that banner ads did nothing for the user. Banner ads only helped advertisers.

And then there were the search results. Larry and Sergey also understood that searches had to be accurate and relevant. For Google, it wasn't about getting people to hang out on Google.com. It was about getting users great results as quickly as possible.

Hook. Line. And sinker. Hands down. It was such a stark wake-up call for web users. Google had fixed two massive things that most people hadn't even realized was broken: the way search looked, and the way search worked.

Google was already innovative and groundbreaking, and soon it was also something else: fun!

DON'T MIND IF I DOO—DLE

IN AUGUST 1998, JUST BEFORE LARRY AND SERGEY OFFICIALLY incorporated as Google Inc., they took a trip to the Nevada desert.

Why? Burning Man, of course. Don't worry. They did not actually burn a man. No, Burning Man is a pop-up party in a pop-up town in the middle of the desert with thousands of like-minded people. And . . . attending Burning Man is a whole lot more fun than filling out paperwork and opening bank accounts.

Burning Man organizers describe it as "a city in the desert. A culture of possibility. A network of dreamers and doers."[15] Founders, organizers, and those who attend operate around ten principles, such as inclusion, communal effort, self-reliance, and self-expression. One of these principles is the idea of "leaving no trace." Members are expected to leave the desert in better condition than they found it.

Screenshot of Google Doodle on August 30, 1998.
(Via Internet Archive WayBack Machine.)

Back when Larry and Sergey first attended Burning Man, around fifteen thousand people showed up. Today Burning Man brings more than seventy thousand people to the desert festival from more than thirty countries.

But before Larry and Sergey jumped in the car, they tweaked Google's logo. Now the Burning Man icon stood proudly behind the second *o* in *Google*. It was a wink, a nod, to let people know the Googlers-in-Chief had left the building.

It quickly became a thing. And why not? It was festive, fun, and Google's users ate it up. Just like that, Google Doodle was born.

You could describe other tech giants as smart or successful. But not *fun*. Fun had never sprung to mind. Until now.

Halloween brought pumpkins to the Google Doodle. Thanksgiving featured a turkey. At first, the doodles only celebrated holidays from around the world. Fans wanted more. So Google started posting two Doodles a month.

In 2001, Google celebrated Claude Monet's birthday. The concept kept growing to include birthdays of scientists and inventors, and random anniversaries or topics like a series on aliens!

Today a team of illustrators, or Doodlers, work on Google Doodles. Google Doodles now number in the thousands.

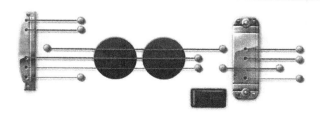

Screenshot of Google Doodle celebrating Les Paul's 96th Birthday on June 9, 2011.
(Via Internet Archive Way Back Machine.)

Fan favorites include the first playable Pac-Man Google Doodle and the Google Doodle that celebrated John Lennon's seventieth birthday. But the most popular was a playable Doodle in honor of guitar hero Les Paul. In only forty-eight hours, users recorded 40 million songs.

Dude, you should totally doodle. There's a contest for aspiring student Doodlers or you can send a doodle proposal anytime to proposals@google.com

CHAPTER 6

Rules Are
for Breaking

NEWS ABOUT GOOGLE'S search spread fast. Lightning speed. Hyperspeed. From student to student, professor to professor, friend to friend. When someone told you about Google, it felt like a rescue. You had just been saved from your own personal search nightmare. And in return? You were loyal, grateful. You never strayed, and you shared the good news with *all* your friends and family.

And average people weren't the only ones who were Google gushing. So was the media. *USA Today* mentioned Google. *Time* magazine included Google on their "Best of Cyber Tech" list.

Meanwhile, Google's competitors? Some of the same folks who had a chance to buy Google? Well, they were burning through cash trying to grab users' attention with marketing and advertising. Even Yahoo! was running national television ads.

Google's marketing budget? Zero dollars and zero cents.

Yet Google was growing at a rate that was hard to fathom, fueled entirely by word of mouth.

In April 1999, just five short months after moving into Susan's house and six new engineers later—Google outgrew the garage.

It was time to pack it all up and move into a real, actual office. And this one was just down the road from Stanford, on the second floor of a bicycle shop.

This meant more room for more employees (including their first furry Googler—Yoshka, the "company dog"), and more computers to handle the exploding amount of search queries coming in each and every day.

But the one thing the company did not have was more money. By now, it was licensing technology to other websites, such as ones at universities. But that brought in mere pennies compared with what Google was spending.

Larry and Sergey needed cash to keep the company growing. But who would invest in a company that was spending money but wasn't making any?

How many searches was Google handling every day? In early 1999: 100,000. By the end of the year, that number had ballooned to more than 500,000 Google searches a day. That's roughly how many people lived in Washington, DC.

Meet employee #20, Marissa Mayer. You may know her as the former president and CEO of Yahoo! But when Marissa graduated from Stanford in 1999, she took a job with Google Inc. as the company's first female engineer. Mayer's studies at Stanford centered on artificial intelligence. Like Larry and Sergey, she loved efficiency. In high school, working at the checkout counter, she memorized every single fruit and veggie product code to make the whole process faster.

Marissa Mayer at Chirp in 2009. (Photo by Jolie O'Neil.)

When working as Google's VP of Search Products and User Experience, Marissa noticed some strange e-mails from one of their users. The e-mail contained only a single number. One day the e-mail contained the number 37. Another day the user typed 53. Intrigued by the mystery, Marissa looked up every e-mail the user sent them. Then she figured it out. The e-mails came every time Google's home page was updated. So what did the numbers mean? A count of words on the home page! That's how important the clutter-free home page had become. When Larry and Sergey heard about these e-mails, they set the maximum number of words at 28. It's often even less than that.

Let's Make a Deal

Ever have an older brother or sister come into your room and make you a deal?

Hey, how 'bout I give you twenty bucks? they say.

Twenty bucks, you think, *I could do a lot with that.*

How about I give you TWENTY WHOLE DOLLARS, they say, *if you do my chores for a YEAR?*

Then, like an arctic wave, reality hits. You aren't going to get that money for nothing. Your brother or sister will control your life. CONTROL. YOUR. LIFE.

Larry and Sergey knew they needed a lot of money to take Google to the next level. And they also understood that, in exchange for that money, whoever lent it to them would want a say in how the company was run.

That made them nervous.

They didn't want any one outside voice to be too strong, too powerful.

And so, once again, they came up with their own plan, one that flew in the face of how these deals usually work in Silicon Valley.

How much money did they need? Twenty-five million dollars.

But instead of going to one lender for the money (which is usually how it's done), Larry and Sergey pitched their company and funding needs to two different investment firms. The plan was that each would invest $12.5 million in Google. In return, each investor would have a seat on Google's board of directors and a stake in the company.

But neither would be more powerful than the other. Larry and Sergey even found the courage to tell these investment companies that if they could not agree to this, then NO DEAL!

To some, this sounded crazy. Insane. The investment companies could walk away completely. Google's future was at stake.

But Larry and Sergey believed in Google and in their own vision of the company's future. Nothing was going to stop them. Certainly not *traditional* deal making.

After some grousing and grumbling, the two investment firms took the deal.

It was time to celebrate. This was a major milestone. A huge accomplishment. Larry and Sergey needed to mark the moment. They needed to eat something really good—and something that reminded them of where this journey began. You guessed it! They went back to Burger King.

Now that the company was $25 million richer, Google could afford to move into an even bigger office, hire more employees, and buy more computers. And the best part was the food served up in the company cafeteria. And it wasn't Burger King. No, three months after moving into their new digs, they made a critical hire: the former chef for the Grateful Dead.

Well fed and hard at work, Google blasted through barriers and smashed a major milestone. Just two years after packing up their dorm rooms and starting a company, Google became the number one search engine in the world.

● ○ ●

READ MY MIND

THINK GOOGLE CAN'T READ YOUR MIND? THINK AGAIN! IN EARLY APRIL 2000, Google made science fiction dreams come true by announcing the launch of MentalPlex. This new facet of Google's search engine could peer into your thoughts.

This is how it worked: First, you open up Google's search page. Next, stare into a special spinning vortex and think about what you are looking for. Got it in your mind? Lastly, simply click on the spinning dial and voila! The mind-reading results would appear. I mean EXACTLY what you were looking for . . . You didn't even have to type.

New! Search smarter and faster with Google's MentalPlex™

Instructions:

- Remove hat and glasses.
- Peer into MentalPlex circle. DO NOT MOVE YOUR HEAD.
- Project mental image of what you want to find.
- Click or visualize clicking within the MentalPlex circle.

See our FAQ and illustrations for correct usage.

Note: This page posted for April Fool's Day - 2000.

® Google Inc.

Screenshot of Google MentalPlex from archive.google.com.

Except that when you clicked on the spinning blue-and-red circle, instead of the promised mind-reading search results, you found out you'd been had. The search results page was filled with links about April Fool's Day!

MentalPlex marked Google's first April Fool's joke, a tradition that continues to this day.

What made this joke particularly effective was that it sort of felt true. Google search results felt like mind reading. And it only took dealing with more than 500 million variables and two billion terms.

WARNING. Watch out, procrastinators! One of the first things Google noticed: Students waited until Sunday night to do their homework. Yikes. Luckily, there are no reports of Google ratting out students to principals!

They could also tell at any given moment what the world was interested in. It was like a snapshot. Today, you can watch queries *live* on Google. The company also released a yearly report of the biggest queries called Google Zeitgeist.

ZEITGEIST? Every era or period of time has its own special feeling. That feeling is made up by the cultural climate, the ideas, and the beliefs of that time. This defining feeling, mood, or spirit of the time is called zeitgeist. A German word, *Zeitgeist* literally means "spirit of the time."

Google Trends expanded that idea, allowing people to visualize and understand current Google searches. Maps show you where people are searching for information about a specific topic. And instead of waiting for the end of the year for this data, you can peek anytime. Zeitgeist became "Year in Search" under Google Trends.

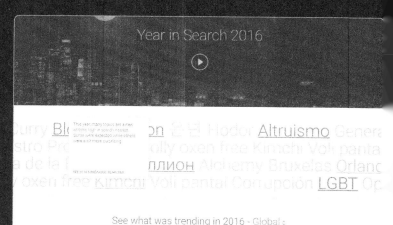

CHAPTER 7

· · · · · · ·

Y2K

A S DECEMBER 31, 1999, crept closer, the world nervously awaited a digital boogeyman known as Y2K, shorthand for the "year 2000." The problem? Well, in the early years of technology, most programmers had only used the last two digits of a year when writing computer code or entering data. If you were born in 1980, it was entered only as 80.

Why was this a big deal? Computers did not know the difference between 1900 and 2000, because both dates end in two zeroes. How would that affect clocks? ATMs? Military missile systems? Personal computers? Retirement benefits? School registrations? Hospital records? Bank records? In one night you could go from twelve years old to one hundred twelve years old. Engineers and programmers worked 24/7 patching software to fix the bug.

Meanwhile, the news media was freaking out about Y2K. The near hysteria consumed newspaper headlines and broadcast news. The threat of technological terror loomed large. It was like an invisible monster hiding under the bed. What would it do? Did it actually exist?

And then, when the clock struck midnight—well, not much happened. It was a dud of a digital doomsday. Now what would everybody talk about? Google, obviously.

While the world entered the new millennium on technological pins and needles, Google rang in the new year by becoming a media sensation. And the best part about the media attention? It was free advertising and lots of it. As word about Google spread around the world through news reports, more and more users gave it a try. And they told their friends, family, and cowork-ers. Google was growing at an astonishing rate of 50 percent a month, every month since they started.

In March 2000, *Time* magazine cried "Gaga over Google." In May 2000, the *New Yorker* magazine pronounced Google the "search engine for the in-crowd." *Time Digital* proclaimed in May 2000 that "Google is to its com-petitors as a laser is to a blunt stick." Yeow! In December 2000, *Business Week* headlined an article with "Will Google's Purity Pay Off?"

And these users were not just Stanford University students, staff, and friends. They weren't just from California. Or the West Coast. Or even just Americans. The trail of users now encircled the globe. By fall 2000, Google had rolled out foreign language versions of the site in French, German, Italian, Swedish, Finnish, Spanish, Portuguese, Dutch, Norwegian, Danish, Chinese, Jap-anese, and Korean.

Today Google offers versions in 150 different languages and counting, including Klingon. Klingon is the official language of the Klingons, a humanoid warrior alien species from *Star Trek*. Hmmm? . . . *nuqDaq 'oH puchpa''e'*?

Klingon pro tip: Swearing in Klingon is considered a fine art. So don't blow it by throwing down just any old insult or you'll find yourself yelling *Qu'vatlh*.

Meanwhile, all around them in Silicon Valley, tech companies that had been flying high were going bust. Just a few years earlier, in the 1990s, technology-based companies had surged to unthinkable heights. These start-ups were often swimming in money. For a while, it seemed like venture capitalists and angel investors couldn't give away money fast enough.

It was a feeding frenzy. Until—it wasn't.

The tech bubble burst. Not everybody could, would, or should succeed. And as the Wild West of the web became better understood, and better used, only the winners were left standing.

The search industry was not immune. As the web grew, most search engines could not keep up, especially those that still mainly used keywords to determine search results. By then, people had figured out how to game the system by "stuffing" web pages with popular keywords. They could even hide these search words in the code of their site, so you couldn't see them. That meant if you searched for "California," who even knew what kind of results you would get? In fact, you might click on a site that is a get-rich-quick scheme. How did the spammers pull it off? One way was to blend important keywords into the background of the site. So a white background might be filled with the word *California* over and over again in a white text that you couldn't see.

That is unless you searched on Google. The bigger the web became, the better Google's results were. The more web pages there were, the more backlinks. The more backlinks there were, the more accurate a page's rank. And sites that were trying to game the system typically did not have a lot of backlinks.

By the end of Y2K, while the tech industry looked like a barren wasteland, Google's computers were handling fifteen million searches a day. Fifteen million. With more languages, more users, and a web that was expanding by billions of pages a year, the pressure was on to keep up. Google's search engine was now a beast with more than six thousand computers at work, crawling the web, indexing links, and ranking web pages. Google's team of engineers pored over search results, software, and every other aspect of Google's guts, always trying to perfect users' results. The search algorithm was constantly analyzed to stay on top.

"I see no end to what we need to do," Larry said at the time. "If we aren't a lot better next year, we will already be forgotten."[16]

And he was right. Not only did the search results need to be relevant, but they needed to be current, too. Imagine that you hear your friends talk about the release of a great new game. You sit down to search for it, only to find no mention of it in your search results—at all. Anywhere. Nothing. Nada. Zilch. Zip. That would be a problem. And a first-class way for Google to go from hero to zero in less than a second.

And that's what would happen if Google's crawlers didn't index the web often enough. To avoid any such issue, Google began updating its web index as often as possible. That meant Google's results became the "freshest" in the world.

• • •

GOOGLE NEWS

ON SEPTEMBER 11, 2001, AFTER THE FIRST PLANE HIT THE WORLD TRADE CENTER in New York City, there was mass confusion as to what was actually happening. Was it a small plane? An accident? But seventeen minutes later, the second commercial jet crashed into the South Tower on live television before a stunned and horrified nation. It was clear: The country was under attack.

Information was hard to come by. There were no smartphones to record what was happening or stream it live on yet-to-be-founded Facebook. The broadcast networks were turning around information as quickly as they could get it. But those efforts were met with unthinkable obstacles from jammed cell phone networks to the loss of television transmission towers from the roof of the World Trade Center, to journalists taking cover as the towers collapsed. It was a daunting and herculean task to absorb, capture, and communicate what was happening.

Meanwhile, the entire world was trying to understand *what* was happening, *why* it was happening, and *who* was responsible.

The need for information was extreme.

Family members needed news of missing loved ones. Every plane in North America was ordered to land. Passengers were stranded. Their families, too, needed information. As news reports began to mention a whole host of names and words that most Americans had never heard before, such as *Osama bin Laden*, *al-Qaeda*, and the *Taliban*, everyone wanted more information.

Whether as someone directly affected by the attacks or as a horrified observer, people wanted details on every aspect of what was going on. That day, Google's traffic spiked.

Users were searching for "twin towers." But Google's results did not include any information about the attacks. The crawler had been deployed a month earlier. That meant the search results were a month old.

On that September day, when the whole world was trying to get its head around what had just happened and what it meant, the Google index was falling short.

"We, at Google, were failing our users," Google employee Amit Singhal later explained. "So we placed links to all the news organizations like CNN right on our front page saying please visit those sites to get the news of the day."[17]

Search 1,610,476,000 web pages

- Advanced Search
- Preferences

Google Search   I'm Feeling Lucky

Google Web Directory
the web organized by topic

Google Groups
usenet discussion forum

If you are looking for news, you will find the most current information on TV or radio.
Many online news services are not available, because of extremely high demand.
Below are links to news sites, including cached copies as they appeared earlier today.

Breaking news: Attacks hit US Washington Post - CNN.com (cached) - Yahoo! News

Cool Jobs - Add Google to Your Site - Advertise with Us - Google Toolbar - **All About Google**

Make Google Your Homepage!

©2001 Google

Screenshot of Google.com on September 11, 2001.
(Via Internet Archive WayBack Machine.)

But many traditional news sites were overwhelmed with traffic. Google's quick fix was to offer links to cached (or stored) versions of various news sites from earlier in the day. It was a quick, patched-together solution to get people the information they needed. And it was available right on Google's home page.

Amit was actually stuck in New Orleans. He and fellow Google software engineer Krishna Bharat had traveled to Louisiana to attend a

As they watched reports on the attacks, Krishna started working on the news problem.

"Krishna started thinking about the problem," Amit explains, "saying, 'If we could crawl news quickly, and we can provide multiple points of view about the same story to our users, wouldn't it be amazing?' That was the birth of Google News."[18]

In the weeks after the attacks, news-related searches were through the roof. Not only had the mood of the country changed, so had the topics people searched for on Google. It was a dramatic shift.

As a lifelong news junkie, Krishna began working on the problem. Krishna liked reading a variety of news, from different perspectives. So how could you put all these articles and perspectives in one place?

"Readers like me, and journalists themselves, could benefit from this, since it took a long time to find out what others had written or said," Krishna explained. "Especially on a topic like September 11, with so many differing opinions, I decided this was a problem worth solving."[19]

Krishna got to work. He wrote math equations that would choose stories similar to the way an editor chooses them for a newspaper. He organized the topics, so that articles would cluster together. And then he applied the concept of rank, assigning stories a score based on who produced them and other factors. Through trial and error, Krishna finally hit on an algorithm that worked. He named it StoryRank.

A year later, Google News offered free access to forty-five hundred news sources. Today, Google News gets information from more than fifty thousand publishers.

CHAPTER 8

. . . .

Rallying Cry

G

OOGLE NEEDED A motto. A saying. A phrase. Short. Sweet. Something to the point, that said it all, exactly what the company was about.

Stanford's motto is in German: *"Die Luft der Freiheit weht,"* which means "The wind of freedom blows."

And . . . um . . . no, "Change the world by making information accessible to everyone everywhere while we revolutionize the web" was not the ticket.

By 2001, Larry and Sergey had come a long way since their days at Stanford, "borrowing" computer parts. A lot had changed. Their homework assignment now employed a hundred and fifty people. They had thousands and thousands of computers at work.

But there was one thing Larry and Sergey did not want to ever see change—their core belief about how Google should behave in this world. They needed to put that belief into words. A gaggle of Google employees gathered to figure this out. What did they stand for? What was their battle cry? They needed a phrase that could be used to test their decisions. An ethical gold standard.

Googler after Googler offered suggestion after suggestion, which were all shot down. Some of the engineers began rolling their eyes. That is, until one engineer named Paul Buchheit piped up.

"Don't be evil," he shouted. Paul had nailed it.

That phrase summed up everything everyone had been trying to say. It became Google's motto instantly.

Larry loved it. "When you are making decisions, it causes you to think. I think that's good," he told a biographer.[20]

And make no mistake, "Don't be evil" was not destined to be a quickly forgotten catchphrase. Those three words communicated what it was that Googlers prized most about the company. They wanted to change the world for the better.

They set the standard high. And they would soon find out the world was prepared to hold them to it.

● ● ● ●

Meet employee #23, Paul Buchheit. He worked for Google for five years, inventing Gmail and working on AdSense. (Don't worry, we'll get to those soon enough! No peeking ahead.)

After Google, Paul continued to work in technology as an angel investor and he made a lot of money in the process. The fact that he doesn't have to work but still *chooses* to is a freedom that inspires him. Paul believes that everyone should have that freedom and that we humans have the technology and resources to achieve this.

In July 2014, Paul visited the Startup School in London and explained his idea:

"We often talk about how brilliant a visionary Steve Jobs was, but there are probably millions of people just as brilliant as he was. The difference is that they likely didn't grow up with great parents, amazing teachers, and an environment where innovation was the norm. Also they didn't live down the street from Steve Wozniak.

"Economically, we don't need more jobs. We need more Steve Jobs. When we set everyone free, we enable the outliers everywhere. The result will be an unprecedented boom in human creativity and ingenuity."[21]

Take that, chore list!

Paul Buchheit. (Photo by Robert Scoble.)

Perhaps Advertising Isn't as Evil as We Thought . . .

"BANNER ADS ARE AMAZING. THE LOUDER, THE flashier, the better," said no one. Ever.

Larry and Sergey understood this. They hated banner ads with a passion.

Larry summed it up like this: "If you had a banner ad, which was by far the easiest way to generate money off search, that would mean the load and render time of the page would increase significantly. We were interested in avoiding that. We also felt like, well, the ad has nothing to do with the search. Why would we show it? It's distracting."[22]

So banner ads were not an option. But Larry and Sergey needed a breakthrough, and fast. The company was spending a remarkable amount of money, hundreds of thousands of dollars every month. Out the door. Gone.

And the only money coming in was through licensing deals— which allowed Google to power search results for other sites. But this money was a drop in the bucket. Minuscule compared with the half million Google spent every month.

This was a major problem. But then Larry and Sergey and their growing team came around to a new idea: targeted advertising. Think of it like this:

You walk into the mall. And all you want to do is buy a pair of sneakers. You have your money. Your mom is waiting in the car, which means you have just enough time to get in, make the purchase, and get out.

But a funny thing happens when you walk through the mall entrance. A wacky sales team is waiting for you. They start shouting. They have on flashy costumes, blinking lights, crazy wigs. Some are doing acrobatics. They are yelling at you, demanding your attention. And they won't stop.

Once you finally figure out what they want, you are stunned. These people are trying to sell you a purple car with orange polka dots.

But you don't have a license, your parents aren't going to sign off on a car, and polka dots have never been your style.

Not to mention you only have enough money to buy the pair of sneakers.

That's what it was like being subjected to random banner ads and pop-ups. They had nothing to do with you and what you were looking for.

But what if you went to that same mall and two or three sneaker salespeople greeted you? They tell you about the latest sneaker technology and styles, and give you the inside scoop on which pairs are on sale. Useful information that saves you money and helps you get what you want—at the best price. Well, *that* would be helpful.

So instead of running huge ads that have nothing to do with the user staring at the screen, why not provide ads that are relevant? That are as relevant as the search results?

It would work like this: You type your search request into Google. Google gives you the regular algorithm-based results you are used to seeing. But you also get something else: ads that match your keywords. Those ads would be clearly marked and labeled so you could easily tell the difference.

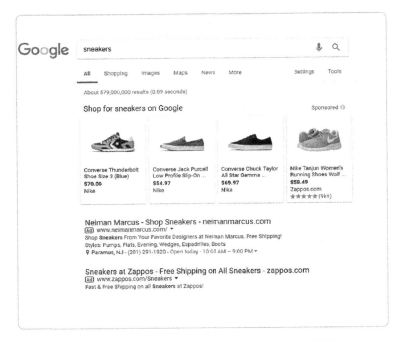

Screenshot of Google search for "sneakers" on August 16, 2017.

This would keep the home page clean and clear of the clutter.

Another issue? Speed. The last thing Google wanted to give their users was search rage!

To avoid this, the ads would be text based. Google's load time would not suffer or be bogged down with graphics and absurd, flashy things.

But how would that translate into money? Simple. Relevant ads + lots of eyeballs = $$$.

And boy, did Google have lots of eyeballs! By summer 2000, Google's searches per day averaged eighteen million. And every time one of its users viewed an ad online once, it counted as an *impression*, or an *ad view*.

Google had started toying with this idea and testing it toward the end of 1999 and into 2000. But like any best-laid plan, things did not go as expected.

The tech industry dot-com bubble burst. There was panic, turmoil, bankruptcies—it was a horror show. As a result, many advertisers slashed their spending for online marketing and advertising. That caused advertising rates to free-fall.

So even if Larry, Sergey, and their new chief of sales, Omid Kordestani, managed to persuade a few customers to try their new advertising approach, they still wouldn't be making much money per ad. In order for this to work, they were going to need more clients . . . a *lot* more clients.

Meet Employee #11. Born in Iran, Omid Kordestani and his mother immigrated to the United States. Omid grew up in San Jose, California. He worked at Google from 1999 to 2009 and again from 2014 to 2015. He left Google to become executive chairman at Twitter. Many of Omid's tweets celebrate Persian culture, immigrant contributions to the areas of science and technology, and the beauty of the planet.

Omid Kordestani. (Photo by JD Lasica.)

Larry, Sergey, and Omid would have to come up with something else as quickly as they could.

Scale

One of the problems of the traditional advertising model was that it didn't "scale." Traditionally, to sell advertising space, a sales rep (in this case, Omid) would approach different clients and get them to spend money putting their ads on Google. But Omid was only one person, and no matter how many salespeople he hired, the web would always outpace the sales force. There was no way for them to keep up.

It's like if you wandered the halls of school with a snack cart, trying to sell candy bars and pretzels to every kid in school between classes.

First of all, you only have five minutes between classes. How many snacks can you sell in a short period of time? You are only one person. With one cart. Oh, and you have to get to your next class, too.

What would work better? Vending machines? You could put one at the end of each hallway. The snack sales happen automatically. And now your time can be spent telling classmates about the vending machines.

Well, Google came up with a similar solution. Self-service advertising. In October 2000, Google launched this new ad service, calling it AdWords. Larry placed the pitch right on the home page: "Have a credit card and 5 minutes? Get your ad on Google today."

Search 1,024 web pages

Google Search | I'm Feeling Lucky

· Advanced Search
· Preferences

Google Web Directory
the web organized by topic

Google Groups
usenet discussion forum

Have a credit card and 5 minutes? Get your ad on Google today.

Cool Jobs - Add Google to Your Site - Advertise with Us - Google in Your Language - All About Google

©2001 Google

Screenshot of Google home page in October 2000 via Internet Archive
WayBack Machine.

The idea was a hit. Advertisers loved it. And for users, it was a refreshing change to get a sales pitch on the very thing you were looking for. Small businesses loved it, too. What if your business sells something as specialized as pendants made from old typewriter keys? Where exactly do you advertise to find all the people who want a piece of jewelry like that? Google was providing that answer, that marketplace. So the next time someone searched for information about typewriter jewelry, they would see your ad. Where big business typically had the money to pay for big banner ads on websites, now Google was providing a way for small businesses to advertise online.

And for Google? The company was now bringing in money. It was not enough to turn a profit. But it was enough to begin to cover their expenses.

● ○ ○ ●

GOOGLE SHOPPING

IF ONLY GOOGLE SHOPPING HAD BEEN INVENTED BACK WHEN LARRY and Sergey were snapping Legos into place to hold their first server together! They could have used the shopping version of search to find the Legos they needed and at a great price. And customer reviews might have warned them about the off-brand building blocks they ended up with (and one day walked into their office to find crashed on the floor in a bazillion pieces—oh no!).

Alas, back then, if you wanted something, you schlepped to the mall or a big-box discount store to find out what they had and what it was selling for. And then determined if you had enough money to pay for it.

Back in the nineties, as Larry and Sergey were busy working on their thesis projects, other developers like Amazon's Jeff Bezos were figuring out how to use the web to sell stuff.

It was called e-commerce. And when online shopping first exploded onto the web, shoppers were ecstatic to go shopping without leaving the comfort of their cozy couch or even changing out of PJs. There were suddenly tons of online stores. But there wasn't a great way to search all of these e-commerce sites for the best product at the lowest price.

Until Google.

In December 2002, Google launched Froogle. It would eventually be renamed Google Shopping. Shoppers could use the power of Google's search engine to hunt down a particular product and find it at the best price. Froogle had an edge. When it first launched, it did not accept paid advertising. It just gave you the results. Shoppers liked that. It was a move that kept the user's experience front and center.

That was in keeping with what Larry and Sergey believed: The user is always right. And the user wanted an easy and transparent online

CHAPTER 9

. . . .

Parental

Supervision

WHAT IF YOU HAD thousands of computers to tinker with, a web to revolutionize, a Ping-Pong table in the office, a celebrity chef, and smart coworkers . . . and then someone looked at you and said:

What you really need is parental supervision.

Wait. What? Parents? Grown-ups?

Well, that's exactly the fix Larry and Sergey found themselves in as their biggest investors spelled it out—Google needed parental supervision.

Fun police: 1

Larry and Sergey: 0

In Silicon Valley, parental supervision, also known as adult supervision, doesn't mean your actual parents have to show up to babysit. But it does mean your company needs a CEO (chief executive officer) to run the company.

Ugh.

That was tough for Larry and Sergey to swallow. Google was their baby. But the truth was the company was spending a lot of money and not making much. That had to change or their investors would abandon the project completely.

For Larry and Sergey, a new CEO would mean giving up some control. And that was scary. After all, Larry and Sergey's vision for Google was crystal clear. The two founders still wanted to change the world. They wanted to do good. And that meant doing what was right, all the time. The fact that Larry and Sergey weren't chasing money made Google a very different company.

Larry and Sergey valued their freedom. The freedom to do things differently, to go against the grain, and the freedom to approach any particular problem with fresh eyes, new ideas, and the fundamental belief that anything was possible. It drove their innovation. It made Google what it was. Period.

Would having a new CEO—an outsider—change that?

If the company was getting a parent, Larry and Sergey wanted someone wicked smart and just as cool. Someone who understood Google's technology, got their vision, and believed in it.

Enter Eric Schmidt, a CEO, who also happened to be an engineer. Eric had an electrical engineering degree from Princeton University, as well as a master's degree *and* his PhD in computer science from the University of California, Berkeley. Before Google, Eric had spent his career at technology companies such as Bell Labs and Sun Microsystems and served as CEO for Novell.

He was an engineer, a computer science guy, a techie. Yay!

A new BFF, right?

Wrong.

Larry and Sergey invited Eric to Google for an initial get-to-know-you chat. When Eric walked into Larry and Sergey's shared office, he discovered his résumé projected onto the wall. *Awkward.*

But that was nothing compared to what happened next. Remember when Larry and Sergey met? The nonstop arguing?

Eric Schmidt. (Photo by guillaumepaumier.com, CC-BY)

Larry and Sergey argued with Eric for two hours, picking apart his résumé, criticizing decisions Eric had made in the past, and then putting down his ideas. When Eric defended himself, it only turned up the heat. Larry and Sergey insisted they were right. At the end of it, there wasn't any flesh left on Eric's bones.

"I was just really floored," Eric told an interviewer.[23] He thought it was rude. Arrogant. Not to mention the age difference. Larry and Sergey were twenty-seven now. Eric Schmidt was forty-six and had run large companies that *actually* made money.

But there was something about that debate that captured Eric's imagination. For one thing, he had to admit that Larry and Sergey were right about the things they said. Absolutely right. And just like that fateful Stanford campus tour, the encounter was intense, obnoxious, but also magnetic.

Truth be told, Eric had not had that good of an argument in years.

As for Larry and Sergey, they'd looked at seventy-five other candidates. Eric was the best. He understood technology, marketing, management, and how to make money. Even better? He had actually been to Burning Man. That was huge to Larry and Sergey. As Larry put it, "He's a natural fit with our corporate culture."[24]

Walking down Google's hallways on his first day at the new job in August 2001, Eric looked for his office. It was *not* a corner office with a deluxe leather chair. No miniature putting green. Not even a shiny conference table. No awesome view. It was, well, it was more of a closet. And soon, a search engineer who felt crowded in his own corner of Googledom decided to move into Eric's closet. It was now a closet for two.

That left very little doubt that working at Google was not about *being* important. It was about *doing* important work, useful work, innovative work, change-the-world work.

As Eric took over the CEO role from Larry, both co-founders had new titles. Larry became the president of products. Sergey became the president of technology. (FYI, they still were deeply involved in *helping* to run the company. And often rebelled against their new "adult," even subjecting him to pranks, like installing a phone booth in his office!)

Google now had 150 people working for the company. And by the end of 2001, the daily search tally reached one thousand searches every second for an outrageous one hundred million search queries a day.

One month after Eric joined Google, it was official. Google was making a *profit*. By the end of 2001, the company announced a $7 million profit.

Mic. Drop.

But wait, how did they do it?

Show Me the Money

BRINGING IN MONEY WAS A START, BUT THE HEAT was on. Google needed a profit. Plain and simple, the company had to start bringing in more money than it was spending.

With brand-new CEO Eric Schmidt on board, it was time for this growing team to solve the profit problem.

Eric looked to Google's data for answers. And he found one. More than half of Google's daily searches were not coming from America. They were coming from overseas. And yet almost all of Google's advertising clients were based in North America.

That was a problem. For example, if one of your advertisers is a car manufacturer who mostly sells cars to Americans, they need to show their ad to an American audience.

This was also an opportunity. European car manufacturers might be interested in advertising on Google if they knew half of Google's users were coming from Europe.

Wow. What if they could grow their list of clients overseas?

Eric quickly handed Omid a plane ticket and a mission: Set up sales offices in Europe and beyond ASAP. That's what Omid did. Soon Google sales offices popped up in Europe, Japan, and Canada.

Google made another quick move to bring in more money. They created more space for text ads on the results page. More ads meant more money.

And these two fixes worked. Those advertising dollars began to add up fast.

In 2002, Google placed its money problems in the rearview mirror. And this was how they did it.

Paying for eyeballs is great. But what if those eyeballs are looking out the window at the ocean? They are not seeing your ads. How would you know who's looking and who's not?

Google retooled AdWords to fix this. The team decided to switch to a pay-per-click model.

When you click on a link in an ad and travel to its web page through a hypertext link, that's called a click-through.

For advertisers, this meant instead of paying for eyeballs, they were paying for click-throughs. With ad views, you knew that users had the chance to *see* your ad. But you weren't exactly sure and you couldn't tell if they cared or responded to it in any way. Pay-per-click changed that. It increased the value of the service Google was offering. Generally users don't click on ads they are not interested in. Advertisers would find out immediately if their ad was a hit. If it wasn't, they could improve the ad and try again. This was a win for users, too. The ad quality improved. Not only were users happy, advertisers were happy, and Google was happy. It was a win-win-win.

The pay-per-click idea was first introduced by Google competitor GoTo.com. Founded by Bill Gross, the search-advertising site mixed organic search results with paid search results. Users couldn't tell which results were organic and which were paid. Gross also did not patent his idea, so technically it was up for grabs (and improvement). An opportunity Google engineers would not pass up.

Going Once, Going Twice, Sold!

CAN I GET TEN DOLLARS FOR THE WORD CAR? Fifteen dollars? Twenty dollars? Going once. Going twice. And sold to the car dealer in the pinstripe suit!

It may be hard to believe that anyone would pay money for a word. But Google saw value in their keywords. If you were a car manufacturer and became the top bidder for the keyword *car*, that would mean your ad would get the Google spotlight. That spotlight was the highest placement of your ad. And then the second-highest bidder would get the second-highest spot.

So when users typed in "car," they got organic search results and they saw your ad (clearly labeled as advertising) at the top of the list.

• • •

Rank 2.0

WITH ADWORDS TAKING OFF, LARRY AND SERGEY thought the same ideas behind PageRank could work for ranking ads. If an ad was useful, people would click on it. If an ad wasn't particularly helpful, fewer people would click on it. Counting these clicks, they could assign the ads a quality score. So when you searched for cars, not only would clearly marked auto ads show up, but the most clicked-on ads came up first.

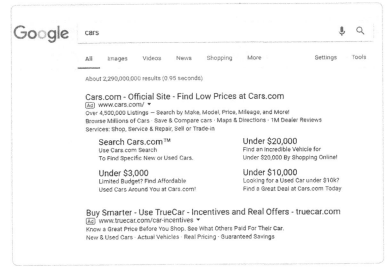

Google search results for "cars" in August 2017.

Now, using an ad's quality score in addition to their bid price, the ad would be assigned a rank.

This was yet another revolution. Before Google, consumers were hostages to advertising. In order to watch your favorite show on a handful of channels, you had to sit through their ads. The TV networks decided who advertised. And what they were selling may have something to do with you, and then again, maybe not.

But with Google, users were in the driver's seat now. Advertisers came running.

By the end of 2002, profits had soared to ONE HUNDRED million dollars.

If you made a tower out of 100 million dollar bills, stacking singles on top of each other, that tower would rise up nearly seven miles high.

Then Google entered new territory once again. What about advertising on *non*-Google sites? What about all the mom blogs? What about news sites? The web was exploding with content. How could Google bring its advertising program to sites like these? Sergey, in particular, was very interested in selling ads on other sites and he knew of a company that was doing just that: Applied Semantics. Google quickly bought the company and introduced AdSense in 2003.

AdSense enabled Google to sell ads on other sites. It allowed for other sites to make a cut of the money. So if you have a site that celebrates bookstores, and you signed up for AdSense, Google could place an ad on your site. As that ad racks up click-throughs, Google would split part of the revenue with you.

AdSense logo. (© Google.)

Google's profits quadrupled to $400 million. By 2004, while Larry's and Sergey's parents might still have been asking when they would finish their PhDs, no one was asking how Google would make a profit—not anymore.

Google had graduated from a school project to a big company to a very big company. And it was going to keep growing and changing, adding new people, new technology. This was no longer just Larry and Sergey's story. What happened next would really be Google's story.

• • •

THE PICTURE THAT LAUNCHED A THOUSAND LINES OF CODE

WHEN JENNIFER LOPEZ ARRIVED AT THE 2000 GRAMMY AWARDS, she made an enormous splash with her green Versace dress. It was the red-carpet sensation heard around the world. And for those who missed it, they turned to Google.

That was a problem because, in 2000, Google was a text-and-link-based search.

"At the time, the dress was the most popular search query we had ever seen," Eric said. "But we had no surefire way of getting users exactly what they wanted: J.Lo wearing that dress. Google Image Search was born."[25]

The team immediately began working on how to make images searchable. And in 2001 Google Images launched, offering users access to 250 million searchable images.

Jennifer Lopez backstage at the 2000 Grammy Awards. (Photo by Scott Gries.)

PART 2

Google It!

CHAPTER 10

Googler (Person Who Works at Google)

FOR LARRY, MAKING sure his employees are happy is more than lip service. It's his grandfather's legacy. Larry's grandfather worked on the assembly line for Chevrolet in Flint, Michigan, during an infamous strike. To fight for their rights in the late 1930s, autoworkers held sit-down strikes. They literally took over the plant, which shut down production. Police responded with force. More than a dozen strikers suffered injuries.

Larry remembered his grandfather's tales about carrying an iron pipe wrapped in leather to protect himself just in case he was attacked by violent strikebreakers.

When Larry delivered the commencement speech at the University of Michigan in 2009, he spoke about how his grandfather drove his own kids to that campus and told them, "This is where you'll go to school." And then Larry held up that iron pipe his grandfather had carried for protection.

This story made an impression on Larry. He fundamentally believed that happy workers were ultimately more productive.

• •   •

Life as a Googler

THE CULTURE OF GOOGLE WAS CRITICAL TO Larry and Sergey. They wanted work to be fun, exciting, an environment that sparked ideas. That's how both founders were educated from an early age at Montessori schools—where students are encouraged to explore their own interests at their own pace. And the Montessori classroom environment and culture is set up to make that a reality. Another hallmark of this type of education? Questioning authority or the way things have always been done.

This was a fundamental influence on how Larry and Sergey worked. Even though the company was getting bigger and bigger all the time, they never wanted to lose their scrappy, plucky, start-up culture. Ideas and innovation would have to remain king.

How do you preserve that? Encourage that? How do you avoid becoming a stuffy corporate office that causes people to wake up on Monday morning and take a deep, sad breath before they head off to work?

Larry, Sergey, and their team had some pretty interesting answers to those questions.

● ● ●

Give ~~100~~ 20 percent?

IF YOU THINK GOING TO SCHOOL SIX HOURS A day, five days a week is a bummer, try this on. What if your teachers decided that for one day a week, *every* week, until *forever*, you could set your studies aside and work on something you were super excited about?

Say, a question or problem like *Does listening to an audiobook while skateboarding increase reading comprehension?* To find out, you'll have to spend 20 percent of your school days chasing that down, which I'm assuming will include a lot of skateboarding.

WARNING! Do not try this at home. Do not call the author with tales of audiobook/skateboard/half-pipe disaster. It's just an example!

But what if skateboarding really does increase reading comprehension? And what if your principal, after hearing your results, invests in an audiobook library and a skate park? Because it's good for you?

Well, at Google, this dream is a reality. Well, not the audiobook-fueled skate park. But something called 20 percent time. Googlers can work on pet projects of their choosing. It doesn't matter if those projects ever make the company a dime. But if you stumble onto something great, the company might get behind your fresh idea and do what it can to support your efforts.

Some of Google's biggest innovations have come out of 20 percent time, little things like Gmail, Google News, Froogle (now Google Shopping), and others.

DRESS CODE: Another thing, you can leave the suit in your closet. Don't have a suit? Don't buy one. The Google dress code is simply that you must wear something. And employees keep it casual, usually just jeans and T-shirts. Some Googlers have even shown up for work in bathrobes.

● ● ●

TGIF

TGIF STANDS FOR "THANK GOD IT'S FRIDAY."
It is a catchphrase the cool kids used in the nineties.

WARNING: No one says this anymore. Although I guess there's always room for a comeback.

But at Google, TGIF is an event, a weekly meeting with beer, snacks, an update on the company, and an opportunity to ask questions. It's often hosted by Larry and Sergey and other executives. And if you happen to be an Australia-based Googler, ugh. Because while it's Friday in California . . . you are already getting your Saturday on. . . . No worries, Aussies! Google has officially moved TGIF to Thursdays, to accommodate other time zones.

The most colorful part of the meeting is the raucous welcome given to Nooglers. A Noogler is a new Google employee. Forced to wear Google logo–colored hats with propellers, they are easy to spot. They always get a round of applause.

Today Google has a staff of more than seventy-five thousand people. "Our employees," Larry said, "are everything."[26] Nowhere is this more evident than in the Google World Headquarters.

Want to work at Google? Think fast! Larry likes quick decisions. "There are basically no companies that make good *slow* decisions. There are only companies that have good *fast* decisions. So I think that's also a natural thing: As companies get bigger, they tend to slow down decision-making. And that's pretty tragic."[27]

Nooglers waiting for TGIF. (Photo by Runner1928.)

● ○ ●

Google World Headquarters (for Real)

WHAT IF YOUR JOB HAD PLENTY OF FOOSBALL tables, pool tables, and video games that you can play whenever you need a brain break? What if your boss let you bring your dog to work? And what if the company stocked the place with actual good-tasting food? You might never want to leave.

Well, prepare yourself for a serious shade of green—because when you work for Google, that crazy fantasy becomes reality!

Welcome to Google World Headquarters. Is it stuffed into a garage? No. The second floor of a bicycle shop? Been there, done that. A crowded office space? Not even close.

In 2004, Google counted more than eight hundred employees. Hiring people and adding equipment all the time, Google needed more room—a bigger building, a bigger campus. Come to think of it, what the company wanted was more of a complex. Actually, what it really needed was a Googleplex.

The name harkens back to that brainstorming session in Gates 360 at Stanford when the math term *Googolplex* was considered for the name of Larry and Sergey's company. Eventually the team opted for the shorter *Googol* . . . which as we know traveled through a misspelling vortex and became *Google*. Now finally a use for *Googolplex* (though, clearly it needed to be spelled that special Google way—Googleplex!)

Google found its new home—a three-million-square-foot office complex located on sixty-eight acres in Mountain View, California.

The Googleplex in Mountain View, California. (Photo © Google.)

By comparison, the US Capitol is a mere 1.5 million square feet. A football field comes in at a puny 57,600 square feet.

If you think the size of Google's headquarters is impressive, wait till you get a peek inside.

WARNING! This isn't your grandma's office building. If you think office perks are slightly burned coffee and a vending machine, prepare yourself. But don't drool on this book!

For starters, if you need to take a break from your work or get to know your coworkers better, why not play video games? That's allowed. Or shoot a game of pool? No problem. The Googleplex has pianos, a rock-climbing wall, a spa, a doctor's office, laundry, three nutritious meals a day, a snack bar, espresso stations, a bowling alley—and it's all free.

Oh, and on Thursdays, car washes and oil changes are available. That's if you feel compelled to own a car. You certainly don't need one to get to work. Google provides biodiesel-powered commuter buses for employees. There's top-of-the-line childcare, too. But it's not free. Boo.

Check out the toilets. Googlers get luxurious full-service potties. Made in Japan, their toilets offer heated seats. And toilet paper is not required. These potties are more like part toilet and part car wash with a cleansing option and dryer. Wow.

Outside Google's cluster of office buildings, employees can also enjoy some green space. There are plenty of benches and tables, vegetable gardens, and volleyball courts. Google provides free bicycles to ride between buildings. You might even spot Google's low-carbon brush-clearing goats. Yes, real (and hungry) goats.

Welcome to Google New York City. Google first moved into the Big Apple in the fall of 1999. Technically this new office was the apartment of their sales team, who was actually only one person, Tim Armstrong, who drank a lot of coffee, so much of the time, Google's NYC office was technically located at the Starbucks on Eighty-Sixth Street.

Today Google's NYC office is home to four thousand Googlers. You can find it at 111 Eighth Avenue. The building takes up an entire city block, and Googlers use scooters to get around the hallways. If you get bored there, no worries. You can stare at the walls, some of which are covered with their collection of awkward family photos. Hallways have subway-line themes. Cafés abound. And a strong sense of humor. One year on April Fool's, the office lost a real, live snake. Luckily, it was found!

Google's New York City headquarters at 111 Eighth Avenue. (Photo by Holly West.)

And your dog is welcome. Your cat is not. Google's code of conduct is clear on this point. "We like cats, but we are a dog company, so as a general rule we feel cats visiting our office would be fairly stressed out."

Dogs at Google. (Photo © Google.)

Instead of a series of closed-door offices, you'll find big open spaces, cubicles with low walls, and plenty of toys.

Need inspiration? Or more smarts? Google brings authors and "thought leaders" to give riveting talks. So far, more than 1,500 speakers have graced the Googleplex with their seriously thought-provoking speeches.

What's the point of all this? Innovation and loyalty. Google believes that a big open work space that makes it easy for employees to hang out, collaborate, question, challenge, and bounce ideas off each other ultimately benefits the user. And by mixing that with a culture that's fun and takes care of its employees, Google hopes the brain trust it's hired is there to stay.

In 2017, Google announced a huge effort to recruit African American students into its tech and computer science ranks. With African Americans making up only 1 percent of Google's workforce, the company announced "Howard West," a new Googleplex outpost for Howard University students. Through this partnership, students will be directly mentored by engineers during the annual twelve-week-long summer program.

And starting in 2007, Google took the number one spot in *Fortune* magazine's yearly roundup of the "Best Companies to Work For."

For Larry and Sergey, all of this—the building, the toys, the culture—was about empowering their employees to change the world. Period.

● ● ● ●

GOOGLE BOOKS

LARRY AND SERGEY WANTED TO ORGANIZE THE WORLD'S INFORMATION, but what about the kind of information found in good old-fashioned books, located in dusty corners of the world's oldest libraries? Books that are out of print?

Google Books logo. (© Google.)

Fun* Fact: Somehow . . . 80 percent of published books are—GASP!—out of print. Yikes, that's all but 20 percent. Only two books out of ten! Eeek. (*Disclaimer: The word *fun*, used in this context, may not apply to authors or publishers.)

What about all the written knowledge that existed before the web was invented?

How do you make that information accessible to all?

The truth is, this wasn't a new question for Larry or Sergey.

"Even before we started Google, we dreamed of making the incredible breadth of information that librarians so lovingly organize searchable online," Larry explained.[28] In fact, back when Larry and Sergey were just a couple of Stanford graduate students, they worked on the Digital Libraries Initiative, a project they abandoned to work on BackRub and PageRank.

In 2002, the Google Guys revisited the whole idea. Only, a lot had changed since 1995, when they were students at Stanford. The internet and World Wide Web had exploded. But one thing that had not changed: the centuries of books that held a wealth of information were still sitting on library shelves. Their words, concepts, and ideas were not part of Google's index. And if you wanted to find out what was inside, you still had to travel to the library to read them.

And *really* old books, even ancient scrolls, are often carefully stored in climate-controlled buildings. In some cases, librarians must look after these books with special care, only allowing white-glove access to scholars, researchers, and other professionals. The general public riffling through their brittle, aging pages could deteriorate what's left of these books. So what do you do if you want to read them just because you're curious?

If the problem was access, Larry had an idea to solve that problem: Scan the books. Digitize them. Make them searchable, readable online.

But how long would that take? Larry conducted a little experiment.

He grabbed a metronome. That's the swinging ~~torture~~ timing device that taunts you during a piano lesson. *Tick. Tock. Tick. Tock.* So using a metronome and a test book, Larry asked Marissa Mayer to help. To the beat of the metronome, Marissa turned the book's three hundred pages one at a time, while Larry snapped a picture of every page in rhythm. It took them forty minutes.

How long would it take to scan every book on the planet? Larry started talking to libraries and to other groups that were also trying to digitize the world's books.

And then he hired a team of robotics engineers. Their mission? Create robotic scanners to digitize the books! After multiple experiments, Google's team finally came up with the technology to carefully, gently, gingerly scan books.

Now you could scan books, but how would you search them? After all, some of the fonts were ancient and out of use, or came in odd sizes. Enter the software programmers. Tinkering, typing, and coding, they came up with a program that could spot odd letter variations—in 430

Two problems solved. Then Google Print (now called Google Books) needed access to vast collections of books.

In 2004, Google announced a partnership with a long list of modern publishers and libraries at Harvard, Stanford, the University of Michigan, the University of Oxford, and the New York Public Library. Users would be able to read snippets of certain books or entire texts of books whose copyrights had expired.

But their *ta-da!* was met with controversy. Not everyone thought it was a great idea. Some authors felt it was a copyright infringement.

When you write a poem, paint a picture, or make a film, what's to keep someone else from stealing your work and publishing it under their name? Or giving it away for free? The answer is copyright law. A copyright is legal protection for your rights as the creator of the work. Copyright infringement is the illegal use of the work that is protected by a copyright.

As the controversy brewed and began to make headlines, Eric Schmidt explained Google's intentions. He wrote an opinion piece for the *Wall Street Journal*.

"Imagine sitting at your computer and, in less than a second, searching the full text of every book ever written," Schmidt explained. "Imagine one giant electronic card catalog that makes all the world's books discoverable with just a few keystrokes by anyone, anywhere, anytime. That's the vision behind Google Print, a program we introduced last fall to help users search through the oceans of information contained in the world's books."[29]

Eventually, in 2008, Google struck an agreement with the Authors Guild and the Association of American Publishers. In a press release, Sergey reacted by saying, "While this agreement is a real win-win for all of us, the real victors are all the readers. The tremendous wealth of knowledge that lies within the books of the world will now be at their fingertips."[30]

Today, Google Books has scanned more than thirty million titles.

EXPERT TIME-TRAVEL TIP: If you are still running the time machine and visit a medieval monastery, keep the Google Books thing to yourself. Monks in that period of time have hand cramps so horrific they make your texting-thumbitis look silly. That's because the only way to make copies of books was to rewrite them by hand, using goose quills. So mum's the word. You do not want to make a monk cry. The tears could ruin the artistic lettering and perfect handwriting.

CHAPTER 11

· · · · · ·

That's No Joke!

G OOGLE'S APRIL Fool's pranks quickly became an infamous tradition that had people around the world waiting for more of that special *Google-y* fun. Jokes included rolling out search in languages like Klingon and Swedish Chef. Another year, Google "revealed" the secret behind PageRank: clusters of pecking pigeons quickly ranking web pages!

Want to impress the Gen X peeps in your life? Hit them with a little Swedish Chef. The Swedish Chef was a character on *The Muppet Show*, a hit TV series in the late 1970s and early 1980s. The mumbling, bumbling character always ended his gibberish songs with "*Bork! Bork! Bork!*"

Pro tip: While British and American audiences may remember the Swedish Chef fondly, many Swedes find his stereotype offensive.

So you can imagine that on April 1, 2004, when a press release announced a new service from Google, people thought it was a joke.

The new service? Gmail. Free, web-based e-mail. Google's announcement boasted huge amounts of storage. I mean, five hundred times the amount that competitors like Yahoo! and Hotmail offered. Even techie experts were like, "Yeah, right!"

Gmail logo. (© Google.)

First of all, free e-mail was already popular. But it came with a serious downside that went something like this:

You are out there in the world living your life, maybe you are even in college by now. And you're busy e-mailing your friends, teachers, boss, coworkers, etc. Maybe you attach pictures to these e-mails. And in the midst of this electronic zen? The jarring sound of a telephone call. *RING! RING!*

MOM: *Hey, honey, it's your mother. Are you okay?*

YOU: *Um . . . yes?* You are so confused. *I'm okay, um, the last time I checked.*

MOM: *Well, I've been trying to e-mail you all morning, but it won't go through. Your e-mail keeps coming back.*

That's when you make a mad dash to your computer only to discover you reached your e-mail's tiny storage limit. Storage limit? Yes, storage limit. You could have free e-mail, but you could only store so much of it. And it's free, so it's not like you could complain about that. Right?

There you sat, desperately deleting e-mails to get back under the limit—while you listened to your mother. Phew! For now.

At the time, Yahoo! was one of the most popular web-based e-mail providers. Its free service came with only 4 MB of storage. Bottom line? You'd better delete-delete-delete your e-mails regularly or your phone is going to ring with people who can't reach you. Or worse, you are going to miss an e-mail offering you an internship or a summer job. Oops!

Spam only made this problem worse. Users might have been on top of their storage limit, but their inboxes were filling with spam. Spam still counted against your storage limit. All you could do was open your inbox every day and have a delete-a-thon.

Like junk snail mail that fills your physical mailbox, spam refers to mass e-mailings of irrelevant, often unwanted, and even inappropriate messages.

So this crazy April Fool's announcement from Google offered an astonishing 1 GB of storage. That's one thousand megabytes! For users? Reading this announcement was like reading science fiction fantasy. It basically meant you no longer needed to even think about storage. It was simply no longer an issue. And that's why some people thought it was a super-funny hoax, a poke at the state of e-mail. Keep *all* of your e-mails for *all* of time? Nah, but Happy April Fool's. LOL.

But Gmail was no joke. This April 1 announcement was about to change the way the world used e-mail.

Googlers had secretly been working on Gmail, a result of 20 percent time, for three years.

And it had to meet Larry and Sergey's standards, which were sky high. To Google's co-founders, what was the point of offering e-mail unless Gmail was unbelievably better than anything out there? And the standard for better? The user's experience. Period.

Not only did Gmail enable people to take their finger off the delete button, but it also offered search for your e-mail account. This meant you no longer had to sift through your inbox looking for a specific e-mail or spend hours categorizing and filing every e-mail in your inbox and sent box. It's something we take for granted today. But back then, this was a brand-new feature. It was also an example of something that Google was really good at it: taking its existing strengths and applying it to something new.

The look was key, too. It could not be cluttered. It had to have that clean, clear Google look. In fact, engineers even decided to go without a delete button because the days of deleting were done!

●　●　○　●

A Google-y Mess

THERE WAS ONE CAVEAT TO THE CLUTTER-FREE concept: Gmail would have advertising. Gmail was a way not only for Google to solve a problem but also to make money in the process.

Just like your search query triggered keyword-specific ads, now the words in your e-mail would be matched to specific ads.

WARNING! Cue the creepy music that always plays when something bad is about to happen.

At first, you could only get a Gmail account by invitation. That invitation went out to technology reporters, trendsetters, and others whose first impression could spark buzz about Gmail.

The spark they were hoping for exploded into a firestorm. The problem? Privacy. The idea that Google's computers were reading e-mails and matching them with appropriate ads made international headlines.

PC World's headline read "Privacy Issues Plague Google's Gmail." Across the pond, a BBC article got to the point with this question: "Online Snooping?" The Wall Street Journal called the e-mail scanning "creepy." PC Magazine's headline "Is Gmail Safe?" might have been jaw-dropping, but the article actually tried to explain that computers don't *read* anything, rather they analyze text, just like spam filters.

But there was no putting the genie back in the bottle. Whether people agreed that privacy was an issue or not, they were talking about it. The outcry was big and it questioned the heart of Google: its motto, "Don't be evil."

Larry and Sergey never saw it coming. In their quest to improve e-mail, the issue of privacy did not come up.

"We really felt like, 'Wow, something was mentioned in my e-mail and I actually got an ad that was relevant.' That was amazing. We thought that was a great thing," Larry explained to a biographer.[31]

And Sergey? "We didn't give it a second thought," he said in an interview. "There were plenty of things to question, but I never batted an eyelash at that. It never occurred to me as a privacy thing."[32]

It didn't take long for a letter demanding Gmail's death to arrive at the Googleplex. It was signed by more than three dozen civil rights and privacy groups. A state lawmaker even wanted to make e-mail ads illegal.

Larry and Sergey gathered a group of engineers, marketing employees, and even a former vice president of the United Sates, Al Gore, to help put out the flames. Calling reporters, lawmakers, technology experts, and anyone else they could think of, the team began making its case: Gmail wasn't creepy. Oh, and about that delete button? It was quickly added to calm fears that Google could keep and read your e-mails forever. Google also agreed to delete unwanted accounts and to destroy deleted e-mails on a timely basis.

As news headlines moved on, a surprising thing happened: People started using Gmail. And . . . they liked it. Since you could still only get an account by invitation, people were selling their accounts on eBay for a hundred dollars.

Rave reviews followed. And Gmail accounts became available for anyone who wanted one. While the privacy debate cooled, it didn't completely die down. In early 2017, the European Union announced proposals for strict privacy rules that would make it impossible for e-mail to be scanned without users' permission.

By 2017, Gmail was being used by more than 1.2 billion people!

Then, in July 2017, Google made a surprise announcement. It would no longer scan the e-mails in free Gmail accounts for personalized ad targeting. That change meant any ads you saw were based on the user settings of your account, and *not* the content of your e-mail. Pro tip: You can disable the personalized ads feature in your settings.

What if you are being investigated for fraud or stealing or some other crime? Should government investigators be able to read your e-mails? At Google, each official request from the government is carefully reviewed. After that review, Google decides whether to share the requested data.

● ● ●

GOOG

O N A U G U S T 19, 2 0 0 4, S E R G E Y S E T T L E D I N T O work at the Googleplex in Mountain View, like it was just another normal day. But it was anything but normal.

Across the country in New York City, Larry woke up and put on a suit. Not his usual jeans and T-shirt. But a suit and tie. Then he joined Eric Schmidt and other Google executives for breakfast. That's when it happened.

No, you are not reading *Diary of a Wimpy Kid*. This really happened.

When Larry sat down, he accidentally sat on a plate full of cream known as crème fraîche.

To make matters worse, this wasn't just any breakfast on any day. This day was going to be huge. After wiping off his backside, Larry and the team headed to NASDAQ, the second-largest stock exchange in the world, for Google's IPO.

NASDAQ stands for National Association of Securities Dealers Automated Quotations System. It's an electronic stock exchange where investors buy and sell stock—especially stock in tech companies, like Google.

As the opening bell rang, it was official: Google offered shares of the company for the public to buy. The starting price was $85 a share. Their trading symbol? GOOG.

IPO is short for "initial public offering." An IPO is the first time a company offers its stock for the public to purchase. When you buy stock, you own a piece of the company. If the company does well and its stock price goes up, you make money. But if the stock price drops, you lose money.

As the stock market opened, the price of shares jumped to $100.01 a share. The world could now plainly see that not only had Google changed the way the web was used, but it was making a lot of money in the process. Indeed, by the end of the year Google would bring in more than $3.2 *billion*.

In October 2013, Google's stock price jetted past $1,000 a share.

On that August morning, Larry and Sergey became multi-millionaires (if you have to start your day sitting on a plate of crème fraîche in front of everybody, you should be able to end it as a millionaire).

Larry Page (center) and other Google executives, (from left) CFO George Reyes, CEO Eric Schmidt, Omid Kordestani, and David Drummond (far right), join NASDAQ president Robert Greifeld (second from right) in a signing ceremony as Google is listed for the first time. (Photo by NASDAQ.)

Not only did Larry and Sergey own a lot of stock in their own company, but so did the people they'd hired. That day, nine hundred Googlers became millionaires.

Remember Google's first angel investor, Andy Bechtolsheim? He more than made his $100,000 investment back. His shares were now worth hundreds of millions of dollars.

As the team left Times Square, with Google's IPO broadcast on the large screen for all to see, Larry knew he had a very important phone call to make. As the team headed to Google's New York City office, Larry pulled out his phone. "I'm gonna call my mom!" he said.[33] Everyone else in the car did the same.

As for Sergey? The point of staying at work on such a big day was to send a message: Google was at work. Larry and Sergey and their school project had never been about chasing money.

Shortly after Larry hung up with his mom, he, too, got back to work, meeting with engineers.

At the end of that trading day, Google had sold $1.67 billion in company stock. This money would fuel Google's growth and expansion.

They might have been a lot wealthier, but Larry and Sergey were still Larry and Sergey. When Larry returned to California, he and Sergey headed out to the Nevada desert once again for Burning Man.

● ○ ○ ●

GOOGLE EARTH

IF YOU WANT TO FIND FOSSILS FROM OUR EARLIEST ANCESTORS, you have to do your homework, travel to a site where early humans lived, roll up your sleeves, and dig in the dirt. It is painstaking and slow. Months can be spent slowly brushing sand, dirt, and debris away. And you may have only excavated an area as big as your bedroom.

Google Earth logo. (© Google.)

Enter Google Earth.

Fossil hunter and paleoanthropologist Lee Berger sat at his computer and opened Google Earth. Without the worry of hungry leopards, swooping eagles, or curious monkeys, Berger began his search, zeroing in on his favorite fossil spot on the planet: Gladysvale Cave, located in an area of South Africa known as the Cradle of Humankind.

He'd spent nearly twenty years at Gladysvale Cave in person slowly digging through the dirt to find tiny teeth and fragments belonging to ancient hominins.

Hey, you're a hominin. Modern humans, extinct human species, and even immediate ancestors are members of the Hominini tribe of primates.

He knew the site well, and like many scientists in the early 2000s, he wondered whether there was anything left to find there. Had the Cradle been emptied of ancient secrets?

For Lee Berger and his fossil hunting, Google Earth offered a bird's eye view of Gladysvale Cave. Berger quickly saw irregularities in the landscape and he began to map them.

Then, in 2008, Berger traveled back to the Gladysvale Cave with his nine-year-old son, Matthew, and a team of colleagues.

They'd not been there long when Matthew yelled, "Dad, I found a fossil!"

Indeed, the boy had stumbled across part of a skeleton of a hominin nearly two million years old. It was an astounding discovery. It would not have been found if not for Google Earth.

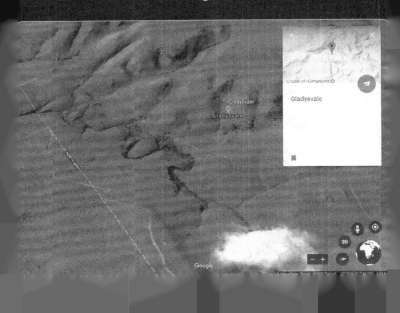

CHAPTER 12

. . . .

Troubled Waters

L ARRY'S UPBRINGING and family weren't the only factors that shaped the heart and soul of Google. Sergey's did, too. He has never forgotten what he went through as a child, living in Communist Russia. He's never forgotten what his parents went through. His family suffered because of state-sponsored anti-Semitism, political censorship, and totalitarianism while living in Russia.

Sergey visited Russia as a teenager, and the culture of repressive government he found there put his family's journey into sharp focus. Boiling with anger, Sergey even threw a rock at a police car in Moscow. While his father talked their way out of a serious situation, it was Sergey who delivered the most powerful words.

Looking his father in the eye, Sergey said, "Thanks for taking us out of Russia."[34]

During the spring of 2010, Sergey relived his family's refugee experience to a *New York Times* reporter: "It has definitely shaped my views, and some of my company's views."[35]

Taking the interview in that direction was not a random walk down memory lane. Google had a problem: China.

In China, there's the Great Wall of China, a military defense marvel and popular tourist site. But there is also something known as the Great Firewall of China. Its job? To censor and restrict access to online material the Chinese government finds troubling, such as searches for information on free Tibet, political protests, human-rights abuses in China, and other information it doesn't want its citizens to see.

There's no question that Google searches were subjected to censorship in China from the second the company rolled out search in Chinese in 2002. But Google didn't cooperate by self-censoring "offensive" material.

But as the government blocked more and more material, sometimes Google.com was blocked in its entirety. That was a big business problem. By 2005, China was home to more than 100 million internet users. And now access to Google was spotty, which doesn't make any user want to log on to your site again and again if the site is down.

Larry and Sergey faced a dilemma. And it came down to this: Either walk away from China entirely or compromise with the Chinese government. That spawned a huge conflict. What about the motto? What about the mission? But what about the Chinese people? Is limited internet access better than none?

And Google was still a business. How could it afford to give up the Chinese marketplace?

Eventually, in 2006, after a *lot* of discussion, Google rolled out a new Chinese-language search that was physically located in China.

In consultation with the Chinese government, Google agreed to censor searches on subjects like democracy, human rights, Taiwan, and more.

It was a hard decision to make, but Google felt that having a presence in China ultimately provided users with access to more information. *And* they could also notify users when the information they searched was blocked.

Even so, Google was widely criticized for this move. How could a company whose motto was "Don't be evil" cooperate with the Chinese government and censor these topics? The controversy lasted for years.

Then, in 2010, there was a massive cyberattack. As experts at Google began to investigate exactly what happened, they discovered something troubling. They believed the attack originated from inside China and that the Gmail accounts of dozens of Chinese human-rights activists had been hacked.

That was the last straw.

In response, Sergey and Larry shut down the Chinese mainland–based search engine. Instead users were redirected to Google's Hong Kong–based site. Sergey felt this would allow for uncensored and unfiltered results.

So did it work? Yes and no. If you were in China and entered "Tiananmen Square massacre" into Google, the results were still blocked.

But they were no longer blocked by Google. They were blocked by China. To Larry and Sergey, that was a huge difference.

● ● ●

BARRIER BROKEN

IMAGINE SHOWING UP TO A SOCCER FIELD, READY TO PLAY THE GAME you love more than anything. Only, there's a problem. You're new in town, actually new to the country, and you don't speak the language. No one understands you.

That's exactly the situation a young soccer player from Spain found himself facing in his new home of Portadown, Northern Ireland.

Alberto Balde was hanging around the sidelines at practice when the coach of Portadown Youth Football (soccer) Club spotted Alberto and asked him to play. But Alberto couldn't understand the coach. And the coach only knew one word in Spanish: *hola*.

Enter Google Translate. The coach pulled out his phone and started using Google Translate. Now the two could talk. Alberto joined the team, learning as many skills and drills as he could. Google Translate relayed every instruction (and practice times to Alberto's mom). When the locals heard about the sheer number of goals he scored, Alberto became something of a sensation.

And soon there were new onlookers on the sidelines—talent scouts from England's professional soccer teams.

"It's amazing what a little communication can do," Coach Glen Traynor said. "Everyone loves Alberto. He'll always be a Portadown boy. He's one of us now."[36]

Traynor made those comments in a video produced by Google about Alberto and Google Translate. The video went viral with more than 1.3 million views. It was even broadcast by British sports channel SkySports.

In 2017, Alberto agreed to join the Premier League's Middlesbrough Football Club in time for the 2018–2019 season. But on one condition— that his team from that small town in Northern Island is welcome to visit him in England whenever they want.

So how does Translate do it?

Google's mission is about making the world's information easily accessible. But the world's information comes in many different languages. And nothing can kill a dream to communicate quicker than an inability to understand a foreign language.

That's a huge problem Google wanted to solve. Google programmers spent countless hours working on a solution. Hours of programming and then more hours of entering in vocabulary, definitions, rules, exceptions, and all the other tedious tidbits involved with learning, speaking, and translating languages. And in 2006, Google Translate, a free online translation service, launched for the first time.

The first translation was between English and Arabic.

Screenshot of Google Translate translating "hello how are you" into Arabic.

Fast-forward ten years—more than 500 million people use Google Translate every month. To put that into perspective, there are only about 326 million people living in the United States!

How many words does Google Translate *presto chango* into another language every day? About 140 billion.

Today Google Translate can be easily downloaded to your phone. You can type to translate, talk to translate, even translate text on pictures, and use your phone camera to "see" real-time translations.

Many times current events show up in Google Translate trends. Get this! One week after Prince died, translations of "Purple Rain" shot up an astounding 25,000 percent.

Google says having the Google Translate app is like having an interpreter in your pocket.

Luckily, a language barrier is no longer a problem if you want to join a soccer team in a new country where you don't speak the language.

Google Translate logo. (© Google.)

CHAPTER 13

. . . .

Verb

I N   T H E   D A R K   A G E S that existed before Google, if you met someone you kind of crushed on, you had to ask for their phone number. They would hand you a scrap of paper with their number *written* down.

WARNING, TIME TRAVELERS! If this ever happens to you, do not stuff the tiny piece of paper in your pocket. It will not stay there. It will leap from your pocket and drop onto the ground in front of other people. These people will read it. And they will tease you. Or—when you are not looking, the piece of paper will make a run for it. Or you will wash it with your pants. The ink will be gone. And when you run into that special someone again, well, it will be uncomfortable.

There were no smartphones, no texting, and—prepare yourself—no way to google them first.

You were flying blind. You had to call them from your

wired-to-the-wall telephone and use your voice to ask them out. (Don't worry, if you're still working up to that, you could pretend to have an urgent homework question—because they'll never see through that.) And when you finally hang out together, this is your big chance to find out their favorite color, whether they are a Squirrel Girl fan, or have any obvious characteristics of a serial killer.

It took several of these awkward sessions to discover the basics about the object of your affection, including which friends you had in common (there was no Facebook). You certainly could not look to the web for that kind of information.

Until Google.

As Google gained popularity, search got personal. People used Google to search for their own name and then, well, they turned private detective, using Google to search for information about their supersecret crushes, their teachers, boss, and anyone else they were remotely curious about.

It was official. Google had now woven itself into the fabric of daily life. This was no longer about finding an odd fact or two for your art history paper. Google suddenly became useful for your personal life.

So much so that even the way people talked about Google changed, because pretty much no one said, "Hey, I just logged on to the Google search engine to query the web for information about our new principal."

No, they said, "I just googled Principal McGee. OMG, apparently she gets the secretary to play the xylophone during announcements."

Larry and Sergey's homework experiment was quickly becoming a part of everyday language.

The folks who write dictionaries took notice. As guardians of the English language, they don't want to add words willy-nilly.

They wait. They watch for how the word is used. Fad? Here to stay? Everyone using the word the same way? Finally, in 2006, it was time to let a new word through the vocabulary gates.

Google isn't the only company whose name became a part of the language. Kleenex, Band-Aid, Magic Marker, and Zipper are other examples. What's a brand name called when it falls into everyday use? A proprietary eponym.

Google became an official verb. Defined by the *Oxford English Dictionary*, *google* means to "search for information about (someone or something) on the internet using the search engine Google."

Definition of *google* in English:

google ◀))

VERB

[WITH OBJECT]

Search for information about (someone or something) on the Internet using the search engine Google.
'on Sunday she googled an ex-boyfriend'
[no object] 'I googled for a cheap hotel/flight deal'

+ More example sentences

Origin
1990s: from Google, the proprietary name of the search engine.

Pronunciation ⑦
google /ˈguːgl/ ◀))

Screenshot of the definition of the word *google* from en.oxforddictionaries.com.

In 2004, Larry was inducted into the National Academy of Engineering. It's one of the biggest honors an engineer can ever receive. Larry Page, at age thirty-one, was the youngest member ever elected.

Verb+

But in reality, the meaning of the word was evolving as quickly as the company itself.

Let's face it. When you say "Hey, can you google *The Sound of Music*?" no one thinks you mean, "Google *The Sound of Music*, but only search for websites about *The Sound of Music*. I don't want to see any images, watch any videos, listen to songs from the soundtrack, or hear any news about it. And certainly don't give me directions to the Trapp Family Lodge in Vermont!"

Nope. In fact, in real life, to *google* something meant to "find out." Your mind never limited the possibilities to *only* websites. You just want the information in all its glory. When people wanted information, they turned to Google. Not Google, the web search, but *Google*, the answer.

Larry and Sergey understood this. After all, Google's mission was to "organize the world's information and make it universally accessible and useful."

And the changing definition gave rise to an innovation story that has played out over and over again, just like when searches (or queries) for J.Lo's dress led to the development of Google Image Search, and the September 11, 2001, attacks led to Google News. One thing was quickly leading to another at Google.

Larry put it like this: "When you look at search, trying to understand everything in the world, make sense of it, organize it for people, a lot of the queries were about places."[37] So according to Larry, Google realized they needed to really understand places. Where do you turn to when you want to understand places? Maps.

Where are specific places? How can you get to a certain place? And what can you expect once you get there? These were just some of the questions they would need to chase down to get a handle on "places."

The company was expanding in many directions at once and very quickly. And this flew in the face of what companies were *supposed* to do. But Larry and Sergey were always willing to part with conventional thinking, especially if the reward was solving a problem or improving the answer to a question.

And Google wasn't afraid to look outside the company for the answer.

● ●   ●

LIFE BEFORE GOOGLE MAPS

IMAGINE THIS: YOU GET INTO YOUR CAR FOR A ROAD TRIP. You've got your playlist, your bestie, some snacks, and a book on how to get there. Yes, *a book* of maps. Printed. Paper. Maps. And you are not getting anywhere without them. Unless you want to stop at a gas station and ask for directions every so often.

Google Maps logo. (© Google.)

Or perhaps your parents wrote down directions for you on a piece of paper. Either way, you still have to read them while driving, or your bestie gets a new job: navigator.

WARNING: Your friendship may not survive a wrong turn at a busy intersection or panic and confusion on a six-lane highway as you take the wrong exit because your navigator messed up. So enjoy those first couple of songs on your mixtape before the whole business turns sour.

Paper maps and atlases were limited. For starters, you had to buy new ones every year. There might be new roads or closed roads or some other change that wasn't reflected on your map.

And what if there was a wreck in front of you? Or really terrible traffic? You'd have to give up your tunes to listen to the radio for traffic reports.

Google Maps changed this for users. Luckily, Sergey never lost his childhood fascination with maps. After all, back in his Montessori days, Sergey pored over maps for hours. So it was no surprise that a company called Keyhole caught Sergey's attention.

Founded in 2001 by John Hanke, Keyhole was a geospatial data visualization firm.

So what is geospatial data visualization? One example is a map. A map is nothing more than a way to see, or visualize, data, like longitude and latitude, even altitude. Once you have the data of various locations and how these data points relate to one another, you can visualize it by drawing a map.

As technology developed, our ability to visualize geography also broke new ground. And Keyhole took it to a new level, allowing users to peek at satellite images of almost any place on the planet.

How did Sergey persuade Google's team to buy the company? During the demonstration, Sergey used Keyhole to zoom in on the backyards of everyone at the meeting! In 2004, Google bought Keyhole for $35 million in stock.

As one of the two people leading Google's geo team and implementing Keyhole's technology, John oversaw Google Maps's launch in early 2005, followed by Google Earth's unveiling later that summer.

In August 2005, Hurricane Katrina bore down on Louisiana and Mississippi. Flooded streets, missing street signs, and damage rendered entire neighborhoods unrecognizable. For the rescuers, navigating without landmarks was extraordinarily difficult. Even though Google's geo team was consumed with the rollout of Google Maps and Google Earth, they realized their new technology could help, even save lives. John and his team provided rescuers with real-time satellite images of the hurricane and disaster area—more than eight thousand images. This helped emergency crews locate stranded survivors, navigate the disaster zone, and distribute badly needed aid to cutoff communities.

But things really got interesting when one of John's personal heroes took notice of Google Maps. One afternoon, John got an e-mail from a man he'd admired for a long time, a man who inspired John to pursue technology—Steve Jobs. At first, John thought it had to be a prank. But when Steve Jobs called him up the next morning, reality set in! Steve wanted to talk to John about putting Google Maps on the original iPhone. John put together the deal.

Google Maps quickly became the company's second-largest product. In 2007, Google Maps added Street View. At first people thought Larry and Sergey had lost their ever-loving minds. Send a camera strapped to a car down every road everywhere and take pictures that appear on Google Maps? Why, that can't be done. Except it could. And it was. And it is.

Google Maps Street View camera car. (Photo by Jim Henderson.)

That year, Google also added traffic updates to Maps. Eventually, you could even choose how Google would get you from Point A to Point B, whether that was walking, biking, or taking a bus or the subway.

As for that road trip with your bestie? Now when you headed out on an open highway, you could sing at the top of your lungs, navigation fight–free. The only interruption would be Google giving you turn-by-turn voice directions and route updates. Problem solved.

Street View gets hot new data! How about strapping a camera on your body and lowering yourself into a volcano? Google talked two explorers into doing just that—rappelling down more than 1,300 feet into a crater. Their view? Hot molten lava!

Explorer Geoff Mackley said, "You only realize how insignificant humans are when you are standing next to a giant lake of fiery boiling rock."

Now you can see for yourself. It's called Marum Crater on the volcanic island of Ambrym, part of the islands of Vanuatu.

Screenshot from Google Maps of the inside of Marum Crater.

CHAPTER 14

. . . . . .

YouTube

N EED TO RELAX after a long week? Want to zone out and watch your favorite TV show? Well, as it turns out, that simple request is a pretty tall order. That's because you've just landed in Larry and Sergey's childhood. Bummer.

Digital downloads? On demand? Streaming? Back in the 1980s, that's the stuff of futuristic fancy. In this reality, the head honchos at the US television networks decide what's on and when. And even then, there are only a handful of channels to pick from.

You can catch a movie—at the movie theater. But you'll have to look in the newspaper to find out what's playing, where, what time, and what the movie's rated. If you can't find a newspaper, you'll have to call the theater and listen to a five-minute-long recording on the theater's answering machine that goes through all the movie names, movie times, ticket prices, and directions. If you space out during this eternal message and miss the bit that refers to the movie you want to see, you have to hang up and call back. And sometimes the line is busy.

But by the time Larry and Sergey turn ten years old, "home entertainment" finally gains popularity. Yes, the VHS player and its less popular cousin the Betamax brought movies into your home. Progress!

If your family owned one of these magical boxes, one of two things happened. Either you were under the threat of death not to touch it *or* you were in charge of operating this sorcery because your parents couldn't figure it out.

But wait! You need a tape to play in it. That means heading out to your local video rental store to peruse its selection (fingers crossed, the movie you want to see isn't already rented). Oh, and don't forget your wallet. You have to pay to rent the movie.

If you find yourself in 1983, check out *The Secret of NIMH* and *Raiders of the Lost Ark*.

There was another option. You could always buy a package of blank tapes and record something from *live* television. But unless you have a super-fancy, best-of-the-best VHS machine, you can't change the channel while it's recording. And sometimes, if you watch that tape a million times, it gets worn out, and the quality starts to slip. Ugh.

Sometimes the VHS player would eat the tape. When you pulled the cassette out, this jumble of unplayable tape had to be extracted from the machine. Sometimes it happened mid-movie!

Old VHS tape. (Photo by Nicholas Buffler.)

Bottom line, watching video could quickly become complicated with limited choices. Certainly not the relax-fest you were
hoping for.

Sharing videos was even worse. If you wanted someone to see
something hilarious you'd caught on camera, you would have to
give them your only copy to watch. (If you could cobble together
two VHS players, you could make a copy, but the video lost a
generation in the process, which meant the quality suffered.) And
if your buddy lived across the country, you had to mail it. By the
time they got it? Moment over.

That's where Chad Hurley, Steve Chen, and Jawed Karim come in (about twenty years later). They were three roommates who lived above a pizzeria and a Japanese restaurant in San Mateo, California.

The trio had just been to an awesome party, shot some cool video, and wanted to share it with the world. But first they had to figure out how.

These twentysomethings were no strangers to start-ups or innovation. All three had worked for PayPal when it was snatched up by eBay. With backgrounds in computer science and even fine arts, they started approaching this whole video-sharing issue with fresh, tech-savvy eyes.

On Valentine's Day 2005, all that brainstorming led to the launch of a little something called YouTube. The video-sharing site took off like a rocket. And the social media part only fueled the flight. The fact that you could upload videos, watch videos, and comment on them or like them kept users coming back, and grew their loyalty. I mean you didn't just upload a video and walk away. You checked every day, sometimes multiple times a day, to see how many likes and comments you got. You responded to comments. You made friends or mortal enemies. It was quickly more than sharing video; it was a video-sharing community.

YouTube logo. (© Google.)

By the fall, YouTube's videos were viewed a million times a day.

The first-ever YouTube video was "Me at the zoo." This nineteen-second video features co-founder Jawed Karim at the San Diego Zoo. Today, it's been viewed more than forty-one million times!

Screenshot of YouTube hompage in October 2006
via Internet Archive WayBack Machine.

In just eighteen months, users uploaded sixty-five thousand videos each and every day. And more than half of all videos watched online were watched on YouTube. And get this! YouTube had thirty-four million visitors a month.

How much is thirty-four million? That's about how many people live in all of Saudi Arabia.

It wasn't hard to see why. You could watch anything: DIY videos, people reading books in hushed voices, videos of Thomas the Tank Engine track layouts, videos of people playing video games, slickly produced and well-written TV shows, movie shorts, musical performances, makeup tutorials, tours of popular (or obscure) tourist destinations, press conferences from 1985, college-level lectures, and on and on and on. Whatever you wanted to watch, learn about, or create and upload, YouTube was the place to turn to for that information and to find your own audience or fellow fans. The sense of community set it apart.

Watching video was no longer complicated or limited. This was a total revolution.

Justin Bieber was a completely unknown twelve-year-old singer. But he made videos of himself singing and uploaded them to YouTube. That's how Usher discovered Bieber, signed him, and then turned him into an international pop star. A decade later, Bieber's net worth totaled more than $83 million with more than sixty-one million records sold.

The media scrambled to understand what was happening. And they weren't the only ones who noticed YouTube's popularity *and* potential. In October 2006, Google bought YouTube for $1.65 billion.

It was a natural fit with Google's mission: to organize the world's information. It was also a major advertising opportunity. While Google had its own video-sharing concept called Google Video, it was no YouTube. YouTube had half the market share. Half! Plus, YouTube had that social element that bred loyalty. Google understood the importance of that and pounced.

In the deal, YouTube would be owned by Google but still function as a separate company. Taking the top spot as CEO was none other than Susan Wojcicki. Does that name sound familiar? She was Larry and Sergey's landlord from their Menlo Park garage days, when they first started Google.

Today, YouTube has more than a billion users. More than half of the billions of daily views come from mobile devices. And while executives of film studios and TV networks initially fought the migration of video from the big screen and the TV set to the internet and mobile devices—now many networks and film companies are streaming content on YouTube and have YouTube channels.

Every sixty seconds, four hundred new hours of content is uploaded to YouTube.

Since taking the lead, Susan rolled out YouTube Red, a subscription service that gives users access to YouTube's videos—without advertising. The service includes streaming music, original TV shows, and movies. And most important for city dwellers who spend hours on the subway with limited internet connection, you could download YouTube videos to watch offline.

Now that people had a way to upload video easily, an audience soon followed. Whether homework help, makeup tips, singing, your own reality show, or fashion advice, you could rack up views quickly. And once advertising became part of the equation, YouTube superstars emerged. Not only did they rake in a percentage of advertising dollars, many YouTube stars sought out book deals, worked as spokespeople for big brands, were paid for public appearances, and found other creative ways to make the most of their huge audience. Some YouTube stars are making millions of dollars a year.

And in 2017, Susan announced another evolution of YouTube: YouTube TV. This service offered a bundle of TV channels streamed live over the internet. It was a direct challenge to network and cable TV.

When ads are automatically matched with videos based on algorithms, sometimes unexpected things can happen. In 2017, controversy erupted when companies like Coca-Cola, Amazon.com, Procter & Gamble, and others found their ads were placed alongside sites with racist and anti-Semitic content that advertisers do not want to be associated with in any way, shape, or fashion. This made headlines around the world, and some companies pulled their ads from YouTube. Talk of a boycott gained steam. This sent Google into emergency mode. Scrambling, YouTube worked to contain the damage and repair their relationships with big advertisers by tweaking the algorithms and adding other safety checks to stop this from happening.

YouTube's effect on how we get information and how we watch videos and which videos we watch is still unfolding. But one thing's for sure. If you need to relax after a long week and want to zone out by watching your favorite video, TV show, YouTube channel, musician, or indie film, or recharge by making your own video, uploading it, and racking up the likes . . . well, what are you waiting for? This isn't 1983. Phew!

In Russia, the day's news is delivered by state-sponsored television. *State-sponsored* means "controlled by the government." The government decides which topics are covered and how. So, what are Russian reporters to do when thousands of anti-government protesters take to the streets? The answer is YouTube. Russia's younger generation (mainly in their teens and twenties) are telling their own stories, conducting their own investigations, and broadcasting these reports on YouTube.

Going Mobile

WHEN APPLE'S FIRST IPHONES HIT THE SHELVES in 2007, the line of customers waiting to buy one was often several blocks long. Some fans even camped outside Apple stores overnight. It was a party and the beginning of a revolution.

Apple's iPhone changed everything. Before that, smartphones weren't very easy to use. Besides providing access to e-mail and a couple of other basic tasks, they really didn't do much. Most models came with a stylus that was super easy to lose. And then what?

With the iPhone, users had easy access to the internet. That meant access to a huge chunk of the world's information was right in their pockets.

Enter this awkward scene: You are standing in line waiting for the new Star Trek movie and your friend says:

Dude, Charlie X could hurt you right now with his hand beam.

But you know that Charlie X's power comes from his psychic ability, not his hand.

Hand beam? Dude, it was his brain. Hello? He lowered his forehead, made crazy eyes, destroyed stuff, things disappeared.

No, it wasn't. It was his hand.

Before the iPhone, this argument would have gone on for ages . . . but now you reach for your phone and the answer is right there. You googled it.

This changed the way people have conversations. Now you get your facts straight unless you're ready to be proven wrong right then and there.

But it also meant people were using search even more than before. Search was no longer something you did sitting in front of your computer. Search was something you did all the time because generally your phone is always with you. And the iPhone made it very easy. And the proof was in the data. The number of search queries generated by iPhone users was fifty times greater than queries made from those clunky, difficult-to-use smartphones that came before.

"It's really exciting to see that everyone in the world is gonna get a smartphone now," Larry said in 2012 in a Zeitgeist speech. "And for many people, for most people in the world, it's gonna be their first computer. It's not a question of *if* now, it's just a question of *when*."[38]

Google launched its own mobile operating system in 2008: Android. This advanced Google's mission of "organizing the world's information and making it easily accessible." Because let's face it: If every time you need to search something, you have to find a computer, it's not easy. And from a business point of view, having its own operating system made it much easier to have the Google apps on mobile phones.

Android logo. (© Google.)

Not only that, but Android was an open platform. This meant people could modify the source code to improve it and even create their own customized operating system based on Android. That has led to innovation and fed a key part of Google's community.

"I can remember first meeting Andy Rubin, the creator of Android, back in 2004," Larry remarked in his "Update from the CEO" in 2012. "Andy believed that aligning standards around an open-source operating system would drive innovation across the mobile industry. At the time, most people thought he was nuts. Fast-forward to today. Android is on fire, and the pace of mobile innovation has never been greater."[39]

Andy Rubin. (Photo by Joi.)

In 2014, one billion Android phones had been shipped. Less than three years later, Android software activations reached two billion!

In October 2016, Google unveiled its first in-house smartphone: the Pixel.

MAPS + GAMING = GOLD, I TELL YOU. GOLD!

BACK WHEN HE WAS PUSHING HIS LAWN MOWER THROUGH YARD A[...] yard, John Hanke could not have imagined he would one day [...] for a technology giant and launch Google Maps and Google Earth[...] he was just a regular kid—well, a kid on a mission. Mowing as [...] lawns as possible in his small Texas town, John saved up enou[...] buy his own Atari.

Kids of the eighties parked themselves in front of an Atari for hours[...] Before that, playing video games was something that happened at a[...] arcade. A fun place to hang out, for sure. But you needed lots of qua[...] to play the games.

For John, simply playing Atari was not enough. He actually figure[...] how to code his Atari 400.

This love of video games and coding was not a passing fascina[...] When John wasn't coding his Atari (or cutting the grass), he spent [...] reading and rereading articles in *Byte*, a microcomputer magazi[...] was Apple's story that stood out and drew him in. Reading about [...] Jobs and Steve Wozniak, John knew he wanted to be a part of that v[...]

In college, he helped classmates develop the first 3-D multiplayer c[...] role-playing game. It was called *Meridian 59*. John and his friends[...] their company on the day they graduated from business school.

Then, as we talked about earlier, John started Keyhole, which[...] bought by Google and became the driving technology behind G[...]

Maps and Google Earth. And if those projects weren't already interesting enough, John got the go-ahead from Larry Page to form a top-secret gaming division. John wanted to combine the power of the technology behind Google Earth and Google Maps . . . with *gaming*.

John Hanke at TechCrunch Disrupt 2016. (Photo by TechCrunch.)

This was John's true passion. He named the new gaming division Niantic.

The name *Niantic* was inspired by the name of a real ship, an old whaling vessel that brought gold miners to San Francisco during the Gold Rush of 1849. Eventually the hull of the ship was converted into a hotel until it was destroyed by fire. Today, artifacts from this ship, including its logbook, are on display at the San Francisco Maritime Museum.

Eventually, Google spun off Niantic into its own company.

A spin-off is like when a parent company has a baby. The bigger company sells off or sets up a smaller company to live life in the business world on its own. And just like a kid needs money when they move out of the house, a new company needs money. In Niantic's case, John was able to get venture capitalists to invest in the company. Google was also a big investor.

John teamed up with another Google employee from Google Maps, Tatsuo Nomura. In fact, the whole thing started as one of Google's epic April Fool's jokes. They advertised a job titled Google Pokémon Master. All you had to do was search Google Maps for the Pokémon icon and click on it to capture it. That was April 2014. It was fun. But at the end of the day it wasn't an actual game. It was a joke.

But not to John. He and Tatsuo joined forces, approached Nintendo, and the rest is history: *Pokémon GO* launched as an actual augmented-reality game.

Gamers got off their couches, staring at their phones. Their neighborhoods had a new veneer: the Pokéworld.

It wasn't just that gamers collected Poké Balls to capture Pokémon . . . it was that *Pokémon GO* captured the world's attention. And John rode Niantic right to the bank. Some financial analysts believe that Niantic made close to $1 billion on its release of *Pokémon GO*. Nintendo's stock rose 25 percent since the game was released. Niantic, as it turns out, really is a ship of gold.

13

Holliambria

CHAPTER 15

Beyond Search: The Recipe for Alphabet Soup

E

NTREPRENEURS, founders, and CEOs often repeat a business school mantra: Make sure your company does one thing and does it really well. That's the key to success, they say.

But as Larry said when the company went public, he did not intend for Google to become a conventional company then . . . and he certainly didn't intend for that to happen now. Google was challenging the status quo once again, in the way they ran and grew the company.

"For start-ups, you need to do one thing well or you don't get permission to do anything else," Larry said in an interview, "but for big companies, it's a little bit different."[40]

And as a start-up, Google had nailed search. Re-invented it. Made it relevant. Profitable. Created a powerhouse. But the company was also doing a lot of other things. Not only that, Google's tolerance for failure was high. The company believed you should shoot for the moon and explore crazy ideas (like strapping a camera to the top of a car and photographing streets); if only a few of these projects panned out, they were worth it.

"There are many, many opportunities to broadly use technology to impact the world and to have a successful business. We try to invest in the places where we see a good fit for our company. And that could be a number of opportunities and only a few of them need to pay off," explained Sergey.[41]

But Google wasn't just picking up any project or any idea.

Larry has a funny test for how to decide whether a project is worthy of Google's time, attention, and money: the toothbrush test.

Think about it.

Dirty teeth? A problem.

Stinky breath? A problem.

Toothbrush? A useful product that solves the problem.

And finally, another key part of this equation: How often do you use the toothbrush? Twice a day (or at least you SHOULD!).

So what other products need to be developed that are as useful as a toothbrush? What other problems need to be solved that come up as often as dirty teeth and stinky breath? In Larry's way of thinking, if you solve those problems, then you truly improve the user's life. It all goes back to that core belief about the user. For Larry, the user must be the number one priority.

Just like a nursery full of babies, Google was an idea incubator. Google's mission required innovation and taking big chances. And many of these ideas became start-ups within the start-up. Google called them . . . Googlettes!

Lucky for Googlers, we have lots of problems that meet the toothbrush test. And lucky for us, Google has lots of ideas on how to solve them.

And many of these problems had nothing to do with search.

It became clear that Google had another mission: improving the user's experience of . . . life itself. Yeah, just that.

Like . . . are you working on a group writing project and need a web-based way to create and edit documents? Done. Meet Google Docs.

Need to store your photos and easily search them to find the perfect profile pic? Done. Meet Google Photos.

Need information about your own life, like where you are supposed to be and when? Which night is soccer practice? Which night is Odyssey of the Mind? And when's the last day of school? Done. Meet Google Calendar.

Need someone to read your mind and tell you what you need to know when you need to know it (someone other than your mom because that can get a little weird the older you get)? Done! Meet Google Now. Technically, it doesn't read your mind, but it has enough information to know that if you are at an airport, hey, you might want your boarding pass in 3-2-1.

Need to get money from Mom and Dad FAST? Done. Meet Google Wallet.

Want to surf the web with Google's browser? Done. Meet Google Chrome.

And the list goes on to include hardware partnerships that launched Chromebook, Chromecast, smart watches, and phones, and on and on.

Soon people began asking Larry Page exactly how he defined the company. What was Google? What was the common thread? What held the company together?

Larry explained the company's trajectory like this: Google was doing what it'd always done, mining the data and looking to the users for road signs of which problems to solve next.

Part of that "next" involved an announcement heard around the world. In January 2011, Larry told the world that Eric Schmidt would step down as CEO; Larry was ready to take the reins.

The new management structure would feature Larry as CEO and Sergey as president, and Eric would stay on as Google's executive chairman.

"There is no other CEO in the world that could have kept such headstrong founders so deeply involved and still run the business so brilliantly," Larry said at the time.[42] "Eric is a great leader and I learned a tremendous amount from him."[43]

With one tweet, Eric pronounced Larry ready to lead: "Day-to-day adult supervision no longer needed!"

Sergey could refocus his energy on innovation of new products, something he absolutely loved.

With huge technological innovations and advances, and management restructuring, the stage was set. But this act wasn't just about search or even just about Google; no, this act was about something even bigger than that.

● ○ ●

A Is for *Alphabet*

In less than twenty years, Google wasn't just incubating its own ideas; it was buying start-ups with interesting ideas, and it was investing in others, acquiring companies and spinning off internal projects that were ready to graduate from Google and become their own companies.

Larry and Sergey wanted to keep pushing the envelope. They wanted Google to take on more problems and bigger challenges and never be conventional. It was exciting to them.

But what they needed was a parent. Wait! What? Not again! Don't worry. We aren't talking about parental supervision. This time, they needed a parent company.

A parent holding company is a type of company that owns enough stock in other companies to control the management, policies, and direction. You can think of it as a collection of companies under one umbrella. This can be an important way to organize a company that's working on unrelated products, services, or projects. In many cases it allows the parent company to focus on long-term goals, while the individual companies have their own CEOs to worry about day-to-day issues.

Sergey came up with the name.

And Larry made the announcement.

On August 15, 2015, Google became part of a parent company named Alphabet. Alphabet was a collection of companies under the same umbrella. Google would still oversee YouTube and the other internet-based products. But these weren't the only types of projects Google was developing or acquiring anymore.

Alphabet   Investors

G
is for Google

As Sergey and I wrote in the original founders letter 11 years ago,
"Google is not a conventional company. We do not intend to
become one." more

Larry Page
Larry Page

Screenshot of Alphabet's home page at abc.xyz.

Larry knew that some of the company's projects were, in his words, "pretty far afield of our main internet products." In fact, engineers, scientists, and big thinkers at Google were noodling over big problems, like space travel, health, even eternal life, and other seemingly crazy ideas that have nothing to do with internet search.

"The actual amount of knowledge you get out of your computer versus the amount of time you spend is still pretty bad," Larry explained to an interviewer. "So our job is to try to solve that. And most of the things we are doing make sense in that context."[44]

For example, what's more efficient? Maps telling you how to drive to school? Or the car automatically driving you there while you study for a test on the way?

What's better? Reading about different types of volcanoes or putting on a virtual reality headset and going inside different types of volcanoes?

And is the internet helpful at all if you happen to be standing in a part of the world with no internet access?

Alphabet was hurtling toward the future. And this reorganization offered clarity to investors, to employees, and to the public.

Larry became Alphabet's CEO. Sergey took the role of president. And Googler Sundar Pichai, who started at Google in 2004, would become Google's new CEO.

Under Sundar, Google would focus on its core business, which is all the internet-based products like YouTube, Search, Images, Maps, etc., and all the technical framework that supports these products.

SUNDAR PICHAI: "The thing that attracted me to Google and to the internet in general is that it's a great equalizer. So, to me, I've always been struck by the fact that Google Search worked the same . . . if you were a rural kid anywhere or a professor at Stanford or Harvard."[45] Sundar plans on seeing that continue.

The other companies that made up Alphabet could focus on their particular problems, solutions, and products. Their missions ranged from making smart home products to solving health-care issues to making financial investments or pioneering big technology breakthroughs—just to name a few.

Larry could focus on the overall business, while dipping into specific projects as needed. Sergey also took on the role of director of special projects, which puts Google's moonshots at the top of his to-do list.

LINGO ALERT! Pretty much no one actually refers to Alphabet as Alphabet (except financial writers, investors, and their friends). Most people, probably even you, still call it—everything Alphabet is, does, and hopes to be—Google.

• • • •

AN (ALMOST) IMPOSSIBLE CODE CHALLENGE

IT'S KIND OF AN IMPOSSIBLE STORY. BUT ONE THAT'S PROUDLY TOLD IN Africa and around the world. It started when seventeen-year-old Nji Collins Gbah was sitting in his high school classroom in Cameroon. A guest speaker told the class about the Google Code-in. It's a contest for students ages thirteen to seventeen to complete a series of tough open-source coding tasks. It would require months of work, with some tasks taking an entire week to complete.

Nji was already obsessed with coding. He read as many library books about coding as possible and searched online for more information—despite the fact that the government regularly shut off the internet.

But Nji didn't give up. Teaching himself how to code and working with local mentors, he grabbed a seat in front of his father's old computer as often as he could. At first, Nji's dad was annoyed, worried his son was playing games on the internet instead of focusing on his studies. At one point, Nji's dad even took the computer away.

But Nji still found a way to complete twenty of the contest's coding tasks, knowing he would be judged by both the quantity and quality of his work. The pressure was on because at any minute another oppressive internet blackout could hit. Nji made it. He submitted the last task and began the nerve-wracking process of waiting to find out how he did. But the next morning? The internet was shut down. Nji couldn't log on to the coding site or check his e-mail. Nothing.

So he traveled seven hours away to visit a cousin who still had internet. But by the time Nji got there, word was already out. Nji not only did well: He had won the grand prize—a trip to Google headquarters at the Mountain View, California, Googleplex. A chance to meet Google's engineers. The international media started calling Nji for interviews because not only was he a grand-prize winner, he was the first student from Africa to ever win.

And during one of his television interviews, Nji's dad stood next to him, beaming. Nji's dad was quick to say how proud he was of his son . . . and a little guilty for taking away the computer.

The 2016 Google Code-in attracted 1,300 students from sixty-two countries.

Image from Nji Collins, source: https://goo.gl/VbnosB

PART 3

Impossible
Goal + Attempt
(+/–Success) =
Moonshot

CHAPTER 16

A Healthy Disregard for the Impossible

WANT TO TRAVEL into the future? Peeking at Google's research and development projects can give us a glimpse of what's to come. If you don't want to know about a world filled with self-driving cars and cars that can fly . . . or a world where even your clothes are connected to the internet . . . STOP READING RIGHT NOW. PUT THIS BOOK DOWN.

Larry and Sergey spend a lot of their time imagining the future. But to them it's not a daydream. *No.* Instead, Larry's futuristic focus comes down to this one serious question: "What is the future really going to be and how do we create it?"

On May 25, 1961, President John F. Kennedy stood before the US Congress. Back then, human feet had stood upon only one celestial body: Earth. With one speech, Kennedy challenged the nation to shoot for the moon … literally. He called on citizens, leaders, scientists, mathematicians, and big thinkers to develop the technology and ideas required to land human beings on the moon. And his challenge came with a deadline: nine years. This speech popularized the use of the term *moonshot*, to reach for the impossible with all you've got. Eight years after this speech, US astronaut Neil Armstrong took that first step on the moon.

Neil Armstrong on the moon. (© NASA.)

That's why there is an entire division of Alphabet devoted to moonshots: X, also known as Google X. Impossible dreams, lofty goals, and seemingly unattainable ideas are what they work on every day. They call themselves a moonshot factory, by focusing on huge problems that impact a lot of people. Then, if the technology doesn't exist to solve the problem, Google X strives to *invent* the needed technology.

Sergey explained what the X lab works on like this: "We focus on atoms, not bits. What we do involves a lot of software but it has a key non-software component, i.e., cars, balloons. We have flying wind turbines. And all of these things are pretty physical, and that's by design."[46]

X is the land of what-ifs. Researchers, engineers, entrepreneurs, scientists, and even interns come up with crazy ideas of how to solve problems such as climate change, global internet access, and delivery of products (from pizza to batteries). Many of the ideas to solve them are worthy of top-shelf science fiction, but with an emphasis on the word *science*. How can science be applied or developed to solve the problem? What research needs to be done? What kind of experiments? Can other parts of the company help?

The X lab is where these big bets are taken. And its workers are not worried about failure. In fact, they embrace failure because Sergey and Larry believe that you can never completely fail.

Think back to when you learned how to ride a bike. When you first pedaled without training wheels, you probably didn't get too far before you wiped out. But it wasn't a complete failure. Your body caught a glimpse of the rhythm required for pushing the pedals and balancing at the same time. Your steering was a disaster. But at least you knew what to fix during your next attempt. Or maybe the crash inspired you to build a robot that would take care of those problems for you. What if! What if the ideas for solutions were only limited by your mind, and maybe not even that? That's the X way of thinking about problems.

"You have to be a little bit silly about the goals you are going to set," Larry explained to a biographer. "There is a phrase I learned in college called, 'Having a healthy disregard for the impossible.' That really is a good phrase. You should try to do things that most people would not."[47]

The Brain

WHEN LARRY WAS GROWING UP, HIS PARENTS loved to road-trip. And lucky for Larry, he and his brother usually got to tag along. Sounds pretty normal, right? Not exactly. Back in 1981, when the Page family loaded into the car, they weren't headed for just any ol' place. This wasn't a trip to the beach or camping in the woods. No, they traveled to Vancouver, Canada, for the International Joint Conference on Artificial Intelligence.

As they approached the exhibit hall, Larry couldn't wait to get inside because that hall was filled with ROBOTS! Just steps away, the Page family plan hit a snag—a serious-minded security guard did not want to let Larry in. It was the rules, he explained. Nobody under sixteen got in. Wait a minute! All that way? All that expectation? Only to be derailed by the *rules*?

Larry was being raised by a dad who taught him to challenge conventional thinking. And sometimes you have to lead by example. So Larry's dad, an AI expert, was not having it. Larry remembers that his dad yelled at the guard and refused to take no for an answer. Needless to say, Larry got in to see the robots.

ROAD TRIP ALERT! This conference still takes place. Every year it's held in exciting cities all over the world like Stockholm, Sweden; Bangkok, Thailand; and Beijing, China.

One can only imagine the debates among researchers at that conference. What if machines could work like a human brain? What if a machine could learn the same way a human brain does?

If you asked a computer and a human the same question, would you be able to tell which answer came from the computer and which one came from the human? The process of determining which answer was generated by the computer versus the person is known as the Turing Test. The test takes its name from the man who developed the concept in 1950, AI researcher Alan Turing.

I mean, let's face it, when you learned to walk, it took lots of trial and error to figure it out. First, there was rolling over, then crawling with tons of unintended face-plants into the floor, then walking by holding on to stuff like the couch. You probably had to learn the hard way that a cat is not a willing walking aid. Then—with lots of falling, tripping, crying, and trying again—you mastered it. It's how humans learn: careful study mixed with trial and error (and more trial and error). Could a machine learn that way? Then what? How would superhuman intelligence be useful?

In the eighties this idea was ahead of its time. The computing power to attempt it did not exist.

But some thirty years later, in a supersecret division of the X lab, a group of computer scientists were trying to puzzle this out. Their project was called Google Brain. They sat so close to Sergey that he could have thrown paper clips at them. But he didn't.

Originally, Google Brain was named Project Marvin after AI pioneer Marvin Minsky.

"I did not pay attention to it all, to be perfectly honest," Sergey explained to the crowd at the Davos World Economic Forum in 2017. "Having been trained as a computer scientist in the nineties, everybody knew AI didn't work. People tried it. They tried neural nets. None of them worked out."[48]

Neural nets? Sergey was referring to neural networks. The whole idea is that you could mimic the structure of the human brain. Our brain is an electrical system made up of billions of neurons. Neurons are nerve cells with an important job: to carry information to other cells. They do this through electrical and chemical signals. Neurons have their own networks, called neural networks.

Inspired by the design of the human brain, the project team began experimenting with *digital* neural networks.

Google Translate was the result of ten years of engineers writing the code needed to translate language. But in 2016, when Google Translate was switched to an AI-based program, the progress was mind-blowing. Suddenly, the advancement that took all those engineers a decade to accomplish, Brain doubled it—and it did so overnight. For users, this meant faster and more accurate translations, spoken like a native speaker.

Sergey smiles when he talks about what happened next. "One of our top computer scientists, Jeff Dean, would periodically come up to me and say, 'Look, the computer made a picture of the cat.' And I'd say, 'That's very nice, Jeff. Go do your thing. Whatever.' And fast-forward a few years and now Brain probably touches every single one of our main projects from search to photos to ads to everything we do."[49]

Today the race is on to recruit the most talented graduates in the field. Google is funding brand-new AI labs in Canada. It is working directly with universities with strong AI research programs.

Larry's reaction? "Imagine if this kind of intelligence were thrown at your schedule," he muses. "We are really just at the beginning of this and that's what I am really excited about."[50]

Yes, please! I'd like to order an efficiently scheduled day that considers errands by geography, carbon imprint, and cost! Oh, and can AI keep a check on my health, too? And remember anything I forgot? Plus, plan dinner? Wait, am I forgetting something? Brain, tell me!

In November 2016, publishing a paper in the *Journal of the American Medical Association,* Google researchers announced that Brain detected a type of medical condition that leads to blindness—diabetic retinopathy. By analyzing images of eyes, Brain detected the disease with an accuracy rate of 90 percent. Brain is also successfully detecting breast cancer cells in research trials. Could these breakthroughs speed up diagnosis rates and assist doctors in patient care and treatment? Can this technology revolutionize health care in parts of the world with little or no medicine, doctors, or tests? The implications aren't clear yet but are being aggressively investigated.

Talking about these advancements onstage at a conference, Sergey said, "You should presume that someday we will be able to make machines that can reason and think and do things better than we can."[51]

In 2014, Google purchased London-based artificial intelligence company DeepMind. This company is credited with a huge leap forward: computers capable of hand-eye coordination.

And one of the first tests to prove it: playing old Atari games. (All roads lead to Atari. They just do.) So if you are feeling bored? You could challenge DeepMind's computer to a game of *Pong* or *Space Invaders.* Spoiler alert: You are going to lose—badly. No worries, it's not you. It's superhuman intelligence.

● ● · ●

ROBOTS + AI = THE ROBOTS ARE COMING! THE ROBOTS ARE COMING!

AS HUMANS, WE ARE LIMITED TO WHAT WE HAVE LEARNED we are experiencing, and sometimes what the people around experiencing. But what if we had access to all human knowled experience? That's a pretty powerful concept.

One of Google's robotic research projects focuses on developin robotics. This means instead of a robot being limited by wha grammed into it, the robot could access all the data in the clo these advances also come with big questions and a debate over called automation. That's the idea of robots taking over thous human jobs and tasks. Take self-driving cars—for example, 2.5 US workers drive taxis, buses, and trucks—will their jobs be re

These are important questions. Sergey addressed some conc the Davos World Economic Forum.

"AI is the continuation of automation that we've seen in the p hundred years," he said. "How that evolves, society, econor social order . . . it deserves a lot of thought."

A lot of thought in a variety of areas. Job loss is just one topic. other end of the spectrum, researchers at Google are askin happens, for example, if your AI-powered cleaning robot m electrical outlet, or teaches itself to clean faster, but in the process knocks over vases and creates other needless damage in your house.

Google, OpenAI, Stanford, and Berkeley are working together to outline the problems and come up with guidelines for solving them. Google has teamed up with other AI producers to think through some of these issues, such as unintended negative side effects, scalable oversight, and others.

Breaking vases is one thing, but Tesla CEO and Space X founder Elon Musk has raised more serious concerns about Google's AI research. In 2015, quotes from Musk's authorized biography, *Elon Musk*, hit the news, with Musk wondering if Google might accidentally create something evil. Specifically, Musk is worried about artificial intelligence–enhanced robots crushing humankind. So, he co-founded nonprofit company OpenAI to focus on AI safety. And he talks about these concerns all over the world.

Musk is not the only one sounding the alarm. Stephen Hawking and Bill Gates have also raised concerns.

Meanwhile, Google and its DeepMind division have established an AI ethics board to face down these more serious safety issues, including talk of a so-called red button, a sort of emergency kill switch.

Even so, other technology leaders, including Eric Schmidt, have dismissed these doomsday ideas as sci-fi fantasy. One thing is for sure: The debate on this issue isn't going away anytime soon.

CHAPTER 17

· · · · · ·

Send In the Cars

I MAGINE LARRY PAGE back in his college days. There he was in the middle of a freezing-cold Michigan winter, waiting for the bus. As he stood at the campus bus stop, he became frustrated with the inefficiency of waiting . . . and waiting . . . and waiting for the bus to come. How many hours of work, research, productivity were being lost campus wide because of waiting at a bus stop?

Surely there was a better way, he thought. This eventually led to his suggestion that the school build a monorail. But it also led to something else: an obsession with transportation systems. As he read and found out more, he learned about automated cars and became fascinated.

In 2009, Google's X lab started tackling this problem. Not just the issue of inefficiency, but all the other problems that come with humans driving cars.

Problems like car accidents due to human error. And then there's the problem of how much your car sits around.

More than thirty-five thousand people die every year in car accidents in the United States. According to self-driving car company Waymo, 94 percent of those accidents are caused by human error.

If you own a car, how much of the time are you in it? Where is it when you are not using it? Sitting in a garage? A parking deck? The side of the road? Doing nothing? Not helping you or anyone else?

And then there's the environmental problem.

"So much of our land in most cities, about thirty to fifty percent, is parking—which is a tremendous waste," Sergey explains. "And also the roads themselves are congested and take a lot of space. So self-driving cars, you don't really need much in the way of parking because you don't need one car per person. They just come and get you when you need them."[52]

It took millions of miles of tests to get the technology ready for real streets with real variables. But along the way, Larry got to ride in one of the cars.

"It's really amazing to ride in one of these cars," he said. "It's just almost a life-changing experience."[53] He's not the only one who had this reaction.

Some six years after Google started down this road, the team made history. Their car made the first fully self-driven trip on public streets. And get this! They did it without pedals, a steering wheel, or—GASP!—even a test driver. But the car *did* have a passenger, a man named Steven Mahan, the then COO of Santa Clara Valley Blind Center.

Self-driving car. (© Waymo.)

Steven Mahan during his first ride in a Google self-driving car. (© Waymo.)

"It's a profound experience for me to be alone in a car," he said about the trip. Profound, because Steven is legally blind. "A very important segment of my life was cut away when my vision failed," he said.[54]

His story highlights another win for this project: transportation for those of different abilities who are not able to just get in a car and go where they want to.

With that momentous test ride, Google's driverless car project graduated from X and became its own company, Waymo.

Only eight years after Google's X lab took on self-driving, Waymo's driverless car logged two hundred million miles. Traditional car companies like Ford and other tech companies are scrambling to catch up. Ford is investing in its own start-up to bring a fully driverless car (without pesky steering wheels and pedals) to the market by 2021.

"It's obviously still a big bet," Sergey said in 2016. "It's got many technical and policy risks. But if you are willing to make a number of bets like that, you have to hope that some of them pay off."[55]

Google has a fleet of cars that are in testing on real streets. The feedback, data, and experiences of this fleet are being used to improve the technology so that eventually a world where self-driving cars are the norm will become reality.

Unless, of course, you'd rather fly. Picture this, you invite friends over to your lake house. A few minutes later, a personal aircraft (that looks more like a spiderweb atop pontoons) zooms across the lake toward your dock, hovers, and sticks a water landing. It's your friends. They're here!

Sounds crazy, right? But flying "car" company Kitty Hawk achieved this scenario in a demonstration in 2017. Larry's fascination with transportation has not stopped and he has personally invested in Kitty Hawk.

WHAT'S IN A NAME? Kitty Hawk, North Carolina, is where Wilbur and Orville Wright flew the first successful airplane trip on December 17, 1903. The flight lasted for just twelve seconds. Today the historic site is owned by the National Parks Service.

Companies around the world are trying to figure out flying cars. A huge amount of investment and research and development are under way.

In a statement to the *New York Times*, Larry said, "We've all had dreams of flying effortlessly. I'm excited that one day very soon I'll be able to climb onto my Kitty Hawk Flyer for a quick and easy personal flight."[56]

Cameron Robertson, co–lead engineer of the Kitty Hawk Flyer prototype, flight-testing at Pier 7 in San Francisco, CA. (Photograph by Ian Martin.)

NOT TO DRONE ON . . . BUT!

WHAT IF YOU ORDERED PIZZA AND FIFTEEN MINUTES LATER, IT LANDED on your doorstep? But in this daydream, the pizza delivery woman didn't drive it over. No, a drone flew it there!

In 2014, the X lab's Project Wing began investigating just such a drone-powered delivery service that could drop off anything from new clothes to emergency medicine.

The X lab drones are designed to fly below four hundred feet and adjust their route to avoid collisions. Project Wing engineers have focused on working through key challenges like quiet flight, onboard backup systems (avionics, motors, batteries, and navigation systems), and a low carbon footprint. All eyes are on Wing. Larry even mentioned his enthusiasm for this moonshot in one of his CEO update letters to users and investors. And even though details are tough to come by from the X moonshot factory, *Business Insider* has twice reported that Sergey's even put his desk in the middle of Wing's office.

So maybe one day your fridge will order more groceries, a drone might deliver them to your doorstep, and a domestic robot might put those groceries away (after cleaning the house, of course).

Yes, please!

CHAPTER 18

. . . . . .

Wear It!

D UDE, THAT GOOGLE looks good on you! We are all in the habit of using Google, YouTube, and other Googlettes on our phones and computers, but what if we could wear it? Think about it. If you are riding your bike to a restaurant and you need to take a phone call, find out what time it is, or figure out which way to turn at the stop sign, what do you do? Put your life at risk by fumbling with your cell phone? That usually doesn't end too well.

What if . . . with a flick of your wrist, a couple of touches, taps, and swipes of your jacket cuff and cuff links, you can take a call, get directions, find out if there is a coffee shop in the neighborhood, or listen to music?

Google has already partnered with Levi's to make a smart jean jacket that's specifically designed for urban bike commuters. It's high tech. Connected. The cuffs of the Levi's jacket contain smart fibers, made of a combination of traditional yarn and super-thin metal alloys for swiping, while the cuff links serve as tappable buttons. This wearable isn't designed to look or feel like a touch screen, but to act like one. This effort between Google and Levi's is called Project Jacquard.

And one more thing to know, just in case a passing bus hits a mud puddle and sprays your smart jacket, you can throw it in the wash (as long as you remove the cuff links first). And best of all, your new smart, stylish commuter jacket will only cost a few hundred bucks.

What's the point? Seamless, ubiquitous technology that blends into your life instead of screaming, "Hey, look at me! I am a cool tech invention."

Take Google Glass, for example. This was a project Sergey was personally passionate about and really got behind publicly. Google Glass was a pair of glasses—well, the frames really—hat had a teeny-tiny computer screen. It was an effort to put all the info you needed right in front of your face, so you could stop staring down at your phone all the time.

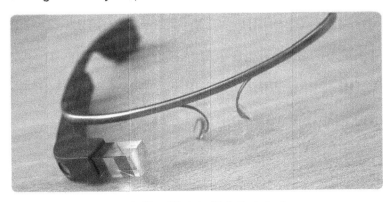

Google Glass. (Photo by Kārlis Danbrāns.)

A man wearing Google Glass. (Photo by Loïc Le Meur.)

Some analysts predict that the wearable industry will one day be a $19 billion a year industry.

Unfortunately . . . they were not cool. They were dorky. And not in an adorkable way. Sure, there were some awesome features, like the camera. You could shoot video of what you were looking at with a simple voice command. Or take a picture by winking. But, at $1,500 a pair, Google Glass was not cheap.

And Google Glass was met with significant criticism. A cool camera feature for some . . . was a privacy nightmare for others. A bold design to some . . . was singled out by others as a showy way to scream out, "Hey, look at me and my cool new tech gadget." Worse? People who wore Google Glass were sometimes referred to as "Glassholes." Eek. Still, Google Glass enthusiasts felt the product was forward thinking and ahead of its time.

Even so, Google pulled Glass from the market. But if critics want to write that effort off as a complete failure, it was not. Google didn't walk away from wearable technology. Instead, they addressed the problem and tried again. Project Jacquard is evidence of that.

Google is also still researching other uses for Google Glass, and some of them are pretty cool. Like allowing surgeons to wear Google Glass during surgery in order to see patient records without using their hands. Stanford is also piloting a research project with Google Glass that would allow children with autism to read other people's facial emotions. The data that Glass collected in the process would be invaluable to researchers. So with Google Glass back under research and development, it may be a part of our future after all.

In 2014, Google also released Android Wear (rebranded in March 2018 to Wear OS), a new version of its Android operating system meant for smart watches.

●　○　　●

COULD I GET SOME ASSISTANCE?

SO DOES GOOGLE HAVE WHAT IT TAKES TO CALM US DOWN, HELP U[s] find our breath, our center, our peace of mind? And can Google accom-plish this feat without our fingertips so much as touching our compute[r] keyboard?

Well, yes. Google Assistant to the rescue. Once the app is on you[r] phone, you simply talk to your Assistant. Need to start the day wit[h] a little yoga? You might ask to see a type of pose, or set a timer fo[r] holding a pose. If you have a smart home, Google Assistant can adjus[t] the lighting and temperature while you practice, and even give yo[u] tips on meditation. If this makes you sleepy, Google Assistant can als[o] sing you a lullaby.

The whole idea is that you can ask your Assistant for help of any kin[d] to set reminders, tell you jokes, interesting facts (helpful to impres[s] people with later), play DJ to an impromptu dance party, entertain yo[u] with trivia questions, and a whole lot more. Google Assistant will eve[n] call you by a nickname.

Google Assistant will answer some questions about itself . . . like "Wha[t] are your favorite colors?" Spoiler alert: They are blue, yellow, red, an[d] green. Wonder why!

Google's voice-activated smart speaker, Google Home, is powere[d] by Google Assistant. But really, at its core, Google is serving up voic[e] search. Instead of typing your query using a computer to get this infor-mation, you use your voice to ask for what you need.

Google Home. (Photo by Holly West.)

What about help in the yard? Something to tell you when to water the lawn or help drive the lawn mower or even a pet companion. There's Google Gnome for that . . . Except Google Gnome was an April Fool's joke. Shucks!

According to Google's new CEO, Sundar Pichai, this breakthrough is possible in part because of Google's advances in machine learning and neural nets. Google Assistant can recognize your voice, understand what you are saying, and sift through information to find the right answer, even if that answer has to be translated.

So where is this personal-assistant-and-smart-speaker trend headed? Google is just getting started. Developers will continuously ask this question: How can the user's experience be refined and improved? Will Google one day provide an answer before you even have a question?

As we talked about earlier in this book, if you sit down at your computer and type in "Why is William Shakespeare important?" Google will give you millions of results, ranked by importance, in less than a second. But with voice search, you ask the question, and your Assistant tells you the answer. Period. Will the next step be for AI-powered search to intuit my next Shakespeare question before it even occurs to me?

Anna, I thought you might appreciate additional information about other writers who have been just as important. Would you like to hear more?

Yes, please.

As Sundar told tech reporter Dieter Bohn, "We want to push the technology at times because you don't know what's possible on the other side."[57]

But Sergey was thinking about these concepts, problems, and potential solutions all the way back in 1999, when he said, "The ideal searcher would be something with human intelligence and all [the] knowledge in the world. Currently, humans have the former and computers have the latter—well, close to it—so you do have to sift through search results. In the future, who knows . . ."[58]

Indeed.

CHAPTER 19

. . . . . .

U Is for *UFO*

U FO! UFO! IN EARLY 2017, high above remote farms of Colombia, farmers spotted something terrifying in the sky. It came out of nowhere. An object in a high-speed free fall, with a trail of smoke. Witnesses were sure it was a UFO. And when it crashed, the smoldering debris leaked some kind of strange liquid.

UFO? No, it was just a Google balloon from Project Loon by Google's X division. The balloons float around the stratosphere, at the edge of space. Also, they're not sending signals to UFOs. But they're providing internet access to the world's most remote locations.

Traveling in the stratosphere, the balloons are flying at an altitude higher than airplanes, birds, and even weather.

You can see how they could be confused with extraterrestrial spacecraft. They look like floating jellyfish. But X calls them "balloon-powered internet."

Project Loon balloon and launcher. (© X.)

The balloons are large and made of fragile trash-bag-like material. So how do inspectors walk on top of them to check the balloons for damage and stress? Your street shoes sure won't work. How about a pair of shark slippers? Yes, that's right! They wear a pair of super-comfy, plush, shark-shaped bedroom slippers that are more like wearing comfy stuffed animals.

When Sergey and Larry gave a TED talk back in 2004, they proudly showed off an animation of who was currently using Google. It was a multicolored glowing globe. But as Sergey spun the globe, the darkness over Africa was stark. "This is something we should really work on," he said.[59]

The truth is half of the people on the planet, nearly four billion human beings, don't have access to the internet. That's a huge problem from Alphabet's point of view. Imagine not being able to accomplish tasks that are now second nature to most of us in the US, like sending an e-mail, video chatting, uploading videos to YouTube, making a phone call, getting directions, or looking at weather radar.

But even more important is the idea that everyone, no matter wealth or geographic location, should have access to information. That has always been a key part of Larry and Sergey's worldview and mission. So they set out to bring the internet to everyone. But how do you do that? Especially when there is no infrastructure. No cables. No fiber. No easy way to connect remote or poor areas to the internet.

What if you approached the problem from a different angle— like the sky?

Enter Project Loon's fleet of balloons. Outfitted with reengineered lighter-weight cell-phone-tower components, these balloons beam high-speed internet to the closest balloon. And just like playing the game telephone, the balloons pass the internet connection from one to the next, creating a network that users on the ground can access through the user's cell phone company.

The balloon is powered by solar panels. It's designed for a parachute to deploy and slow the balloon down as it descends to Earth. The inside of the balloon contains the modified cell tower equipment that's encased in the "flight capsule."

The balloons only last for a limited time. As of the writing of this book, the longest flight was just over six months. So each balloon is outfitted with a GPS tracker so it can be picked up once it lands. (The GPS is also helpful in working with local air controllers to avoid interfering with airplanes!) And Project Loon has its own autolauncher to send more balloons up as they're needed, sometimes as often as every thirty minutes.

AI improves flight navigation algorithms for Project Loon, which means Google can have fewer balloons in the air and exercise greater control over the balloons' flight paths.

But despite the advances already made, Project Loon hasn't fully left the nest. Still in the testing phase, the team is working on improving navigation, service coverage, and other aspects of the project.

The project was still in testing in summer 2017 when Hurricane Maria plunged Puerto Rico into darkness. Loss of power and internet access left the island cut off from the rest of the world. Enter Project Loon.

By October, the project's engineers were directing machine-learning powered balloons over Puerto Rico. Within a month, more than 100,000 users finally had access to the web. And as of the writing of this book, that number doubled and continues to grow.

In the meantime, if you have a UFO crash-land in your back-yard, you might want to see if it belongs to Google!

According to the American Wind Energy Association, only 4 percent of the United States' electricity is generated from wind power. Wind turbines are often limited by weather. Is the wind blowing and how fast and for how long?

How do you access stronger winds?

Project Makani is Alphabet's answer. It is a clean-energy project using wind turbine kites to generate electricity and send it back to the power grid through a tether. The kites fly at much higher altitudes to access faster winds. Another advantage? Kites are cheaper to install, maintain, and operate than wind turbines.

● ● ●

Shoot for the Moon

NO, REALLY, SHOOT FOR THE MOON! THE ACTUAL moon—well, except getting there can be tough. Space travel is dangerous, technologically challenging, and expensive.

On July 20, 1969, when Neil Armstrong first took that giant leap for humankind by stepping onto the moon, he sent hordes of the world's scientists, researchers, engineers, and everyday citizens into an ecstatic frenzy of triumph. And no wonder, humans overcame enormous engineering, mathematical, and economic obstacles to put a human being on the moon.

This feat was the result of years of research, innovation, massive budgets, and the sheer dedication of the people involved. It was also the result of a super-heated space race. Russia and the United States and their government-funded space agencies were in the fight of their lives to be the first to put a man on the moon.

Decades later, a new lunar contest has shaped up to answer this question: Which private company will be the first to land on the moon?

In September 2007, Google and the XPRIZE Foundation teamed up to announce the Google Lunar X Prize. This wasn't your grandma's space race between governments. Instead, this Google-sponsored competition challenged privately funded teams to send a robot to the moon.

Some prize fans and media quickly gave the Google Lunar X Prize a snappy nickname: Moon 2.0.

The first team to land their robot on the moon, travel at least five hundred meters across the lunar surface, and then beam high-definition video back to Earth would win $20 million. Second-place winnings were $5 million. Bonus prizes for technical innovations added up to another $5 million.

The XPRIZE Foundation is the brainchild of Peter Diamandis. Peter has a medical degree from Harvard Medical School and a degree in molecular genetics and aerospace engineering from MIT. Inspiring a new generation of space exploration is the goal of the Google Lunar X Prize. But the XPRIZE Foundation also holds huge contests in other areas like education, ocean exploration, climate change, and others. What do the contests have in common? A goal to push the boundaries of human potential by solving big problems.

Peter Diamandis in ZERO-G. (© Pdiamandis.)

If you could leave something behind on the moon, what would your lunar legacy include? Students ages eight to seventeen had the chance to answer that question as part of the Google Lunar X Prize for Kids. Contestants produced a two-minute video explaining their answers. The winning teams made it to the next phase of the challenge: build a simulated robotic lunar mission!

A decade later, in 2018, the Lunar XPRIZE team announced the prize would go unclaimed. Despite enormous progress, none of the teams would make the deadline. But as Larry likes to say— you don't ever fail completely. And one win they claim? The prize itself changed the way people think about who can travel to the moon. Instead of a few governments staking exclusive claim on moon landings, now it's accepted that private companies could explore the moon.

The teams will carry on with their missions and both Google and the XPRIZE team plan to cheer them on.

In a separate effort, Google is participating in space exploration by partnering with NASA to produce 3-D maps of the moon and Mars with real-time weather visualization data.

In 2014, Google signed a sixty-year lease for a NASA airfield in San Francisco, immediately adjacent to the Googleplex. Only a couple of clues about Google's plans for the site have emerged. According to NASA, the airfield and three hangars will be used for "research, development, assembly, and testing in the areas of space exploration, aviation, rover/robotics, and other emerging technologies."

Hangar One at Moffett Field, California, in 1999.
(Photo courtesy of NASA Ames Research Center.)

Sergey Brin, space tourist? In 2008, Sergey plunked down $5 million, an investment in space tourism company Space Adventures. Sergey said at the time, "I am a big believer in the exploration and commercial development of the space frontier, and am looking forward to the possibility of going into space."[60] That investment will also secure Sergey's seat on a space trip in the future.

Just three years later, the British newspaper the *Guardian* reported that Sergey is allegedly using one of the hangars to build the largest airship in the world: a blimp. Reporter Mark Harris quoted a source as saying the blimp will be almost two hundred meters long (as long as Seattle's Space Needle is tall) and would ferry humanitarian aid like food and first aid to remote areas.

When not delivering food to disaster-stricken areas, the Sergey-funded blimp would reportedly be used for super-luxury travel for Sergey and his guests.

Good news is—there won't be any hiding that test flight!

Sergey isn't the only Google founder putting his money behind flights of fancy or fancy flights.

What if you could mine asteroids for gold, platinum, and even rocket fuel? In 2012, Larry personally invested in a company that hopes to do just that! The plan goes like this: Launch telescopes to search for resource-rich asteroids, then robotic ships will mine the asteroids. How soon could humans mine space? The folks at Planetary Resources are targeting 2027.

DÉJÀ VU ALERT! The name of a Planetary Resources Inc. founder has a familiar ring to it. It's none other than Peter Diamandis of the XPRIZE Foundation.

• •   •

Eternal Life: The Final Frontier

healthier? Aging, sickness, and death are huge problems that more than meet the toothbrush test.

In 2013, Larry and Sergey founded Calico. It's a company inside Alphabet that deals with expanding our limited human life spans. Yes, you read that right. They are trying to solve the pesky problem of aging.

The focus is on genetics and drug research. When Calico was announced, Larry made the goal clear. "Illness and aging affect all our families," he said. "With some longer-term, moonshot thinking around health care and biotechnology, I believe we can improve millions of lives."[61]

For Sergey, there was also personal motivation, especially with the genetic component. Through genetic testing, Sergey discovered he has a genetic mutation that increases his risk for developing Parkinson's disease. It was a disease he knew well because his mother, Eugenia, was diagnosed with it.

He became curious about modifying his diet, ramping up exercise, and drinking lots of green tea to reduce his chances of developing Parkinson's. What if the rest of the world had that kind of information about themselves? What changes might they make to improve their own chances of living longer, healthier lives?

The specifics of Calico's work are still closely guarded secrets. But Larry has gathered leading scientists and experts. And Calico has more than a billion dollars in funding . . . *and* a lot of naked mole rats.

Wait, what? Yes, that's one of the only reported clues that's leaked out about Calico's life-extending efforts. The company apparently has a colony of naked mole rats that are studied from the moment these funny-looking mammals are born until they die. What's that have to do with anything? The rumor is that Calico researchers are searching for the biomarkers that regulate aging. Could that hold the answer to stopping the whole process? Who knows what Calico will ultimately discover or contribute, but this Google company will be a fun one to watch.

This much we know for sure: Larry's goal for the company is to expand the human life span by a hundred years. Now, what will we do with all that extra time?

• • ⋅ •

A naked mole rat. (Photo by Neil Bromhall.)

VERILY WE GO ALONG

CALICO IS NOT GOOGLE'S ONLY HEALTH EFFORT. MEET ALPHABET subsidiary Verily. Launched in 2015, Verily announced its Study Watch just two years later. This smart watch is no fashion accessory, but rather a health monitor. It records various medical data as users wear it.

Not available for sale to the public, this watch is being used for Parkinson's disease research. Some ten thousand volunteers have been tasked with wearing the watch around the clock for five years; their data is sent directly to the cloud. Researchers hope this amount of data will reveal secrets of Parkinson's progression.

Verily is also joining with Stanford and Duke University in Project Baseline to study the population at large, using another group of ten thousand volunteers tracking everything about their diet, environment, exercise, and more to understand more about health and to map it over a lifetime.

Those are long-term projects. But Verily is also tackling more immediate solutions to health problems. Like what do you do if you develop severe hand tremors and can no longer feed yourself? Meet Verily's Liftware, a technology-infused eating utensil. Liftware steadies itself and allows people who otherwise would have to be fed by another person to feed themselves.

And remember how Google's AI research aided in identifying diabetic retinopathy? Verily is taking Google Research's work on that project and partnering with Nikon to assist physicians with additional imaging options to diagnose the disease with greater ease.

Verily's working on many other projects and problems. But there seems to be a common thread: innovation + data. And Google's pretty comfortable in both those arenas.

So, will technological advances + big data = precision medicine and break new ground in preventative care? And could looking at health by poring over massive amounts of new data lead to breakthroughs? That's Google's big bet with Verily.

CHAPTER 20

The More We Change, the More We Stay the Same

W HEN LARRY AND Sergey were both in elementary school, sitting down in front of their new computers, they had no idea where technology would take them. They just followed their own interests: math, engineering, maps, computers, and solving problems. And they didn't let fear of failure hold them back, either.

Years later, Larry returned to the University of Michigan as a tech behemoth to offer the graduating class advice as their commencement speaker. His message? Don't be afraid of failure. Don't be afraid of testing out crazy ideas. "Since no one else is crazy enough to do it, you have little competition," he said. "Don't give up on your dream. The world needs you all."[62]

And the opportunities are huge. "The more I learn about technology," Larry revealed during a TED talk, "the more I realize I don't know."[63]

As for Sergey, when he thinks about all that's happened: "There is a huge amount of luck there. But the luck also comes from taking many shots, so many failures. If I told you all the dumb things I did, we'd have to have a much longer session."[64]

Sergey also feels strongly that kids should take chances and pursue their dreams. "And try to silence out the voices that say, 'Well, there are actually a thousand start-ups trying to do what you are doing,'"[65] he says, because your start-up, your particular effort might be the one that pays off. Or perhaps you'll learn something that will pay off during your next project.

They've always felt this way and that hasn't changed.

What's that saying? The more things change, the more they stay the same? Twenty years after Larry and Sergey launched BackRub, they gave a rare interview together. And that's when you see it. That despite changing the world and achieving unfathomable success, they are still LarryandSergey.

On the stage with one of the largest tech investors in the industry, Larry and Sergey are being interviewed in front of a full house. As the interview wraps up, the two founders take a question from the audience:

Audience Member: *Have you fundamentally disagreed on something at all over the last fifteen years. And how do you resolve it?*

Sergey: *Oh, where do I start?*

Larry: *No.*

Sergey: *What are you talking about? We disagree all the time.*

Larry: *Not fundamentally.*

Sergey: *No, no. We really disagree.*[66]

They both laugh. And the audience laughs with them.

(Photo by Tim Mosenfelder.)

NAME: Larry Page

NET WORTH: More than $45 billion (as of 2017)

DEGREE STATUS: Honorary Doctor of Engineering from University of Michigan. Honorary MBA from IE Business School. Still no Stanford degree. (Mom no longer asks about it.)

(Photo by Bloomberg.)

NAME: Sergey Brin

NET WORTH: More than $44 billion (as of 2017)

DEGREE STATUS: Honorary MBA from IE Business School. As of 2017, Sergey still plans to finish his Stanford PhD one day.

SOURCE NOTES

1. CNBC, "Google's Sergey Brin."

2. Levy, *In the Plex.*

3. Levy, *In the Plex.*

4. Battelle, "The Birth of Google."

5. Levy, *In the Plex.*

6. Brin, "Remembering Rajeev."

7. GarrettFrench, "Craig Silverstein 1."

8. Startup Cat, "Google Founders Interview."

9. Beahm, *The Google Boys.*

10. Hamen, *Google: The Company and Its Founders.*

11. Brandt, *The Google Guys.*

12. Levy, *In the Plex.*

13. Battelle, *The Search.*

14. Page, Google+Post.

15. *Burning Man.*

16. Specter, "Search and Deploy."

17. Google, "The Evolution of Search."

18. Google, "The Evolution of Search."

19. Vise and Malseed. *The Google Story.*

20. Buchheit, "The Technology."

21. Battelle, *The Search.*

22. Battelle, *The Search.*

23. Battelle, *The Search.*

24. Google, "Google Names Dr. Eric Schmidt."

25. Reed, "Jennifer Lopez's Famous Grammys Dress."

26. Brin and Page. "2004 Founders' IPO Letter."

27. Beahm, *The Google Boys.*

28. Google, "Google Checks Out Library Books."

29. Schmidt, "Books of Revelation."

30. Beahm, *The Google Boys.*

31. Levy, *In the Plex.*

32. Levy, *In the Plex.*

33. Auletta, *Googled.*

34. Malseed, "The Story of Sergey Brin."

35. Lohr, "Interview."

36. Turovsky, "Fútbol, Translated."

37. Startup Cat, "Google Founders Interview."

38. Beahm, *The Google Boys.*

39. Beahm, *The Google Boys.*

40. Startup Cat, "Google Founders Interview."

41. Startup Cat, "Google Founders Interview."

42. Sullivan, "Was It Time for a Fresh Face?"

43. Startup Cat, "Google Founders Interview."

44. Startup Cat, "Google Founders Interview."

45. Bohn, "Chasing the Next Billion."

46. Startup Cat, "Google Founders Interview."

47. Isaacson, *The Innovators.*

48. World Economic Forum, "Davos 2017."

49. World Economic Forum, "Davos 2017."

50. Page, "Where's Google Going Next?"

51. Startup Cat, "Google Founders Interview."

52. Startup Cat, "Google Founders Interview."

53. Beahm, *The Google Boys.*

54. Waymo, "Say Hello to Waymo."

55. Startup Cat, "Google Founders Interview."

56. Markoff, "No Longer a Dream."

57. Bohn, "Slamdance."

58. Beahm, *The Google Boys.*

59. Brin and Page. "The Genesis of Google."

60. Schwartz, "Google Co-Founder Books a Space Flight."

61. Google, "Google Announces Calico."

62. Google, "Larry Page's University of Michigan Commencement Address."

63. Brin and Page, "The Genesis of Google."

64. World Economic Forum, "Davos 2017."

65. World Economic Forum, "Davos 2017."

66. Startup Cat, "Google Founders Interview."

BIBLIOGRAPHY

Adib, Desiree. "Pop Star Justin Bieber Is on the Brink of Superstardom." *ABC News* online, November 14, 2009. http://abcnews.go.com/GMA/Weekend/teen-pop-star-justin-bieber-discovered-youtube/story?id=9068403.

Aronson, Marc, and Lee R. Berger. *The Skull in the Rock: How a Scientist, a Boy, and Google Earth Opened a New Window on Human Origins.* Washington, DC: National Geographic Society, 2012.

Associated Press. "Google Agrees to Censor Results in China." *NBC News* online, January 25, 2006. http://www.nbcnews.com/id/11012756/ns/technology_and_science-tech_and_gadgets/t/google-agrees-censor-results-china.

Associated Press. "Tech Tycoons in Asteroid Mining Venture." Space, *Guardian*, April 24, 2012. https://www.theguardian.com/science/2012/apr/24/tech-tycoons-asteroid-mining-venture.

Auletta, Ken. *Googled: The End of the World as We Know It.* New York: Penguin, 2009.

Battelle, John. "The Birth of Google." Wired.com, August 1, 2005. http://www.wired.com/2005/08/battelle.

Battelle, John. *The Search: How Google and Its Rivals Rewrote the Rules of Business and Transformed Our Culture.* New York: Penguin Group, 2005.

BBC News online. "Google Balloon Mistaken for UFO as It Crashes in Colombia." March 14, 2017. http://www.bbc.com/news/world-latin-america-39265813.

BBC News online. "Google Coding Champion Whose Cameroon Hometown Is Cut Off from the Internet." February 10, 2017. http://www.bbc.com/news/world-africa-38922819.

BBC News online. "Google's Gmail Sparks Privacy Row." April 5, 2004. http://news.bbc.co.uk/2/hi/business/3602745.stm.

Beahm, George, ed. *The Google Boys: Sergey Brin and Larry Page in Their Own Words.* Chicago: B2 Books, An Agate Imprint, 2014.

Bennett, Jay. "First Private Moon Landing Gears Up for Launch by Year's End." *Popular Mechanics*, June 2, 2017. http://www.popularmechanics.com/space/moon-mars/a26702/moon-express-lunar-landing-launch-years-end.

Biography.com. "Nikola Tesla." Last modified July 10, 2017. http://www.biography.com/people/nikola-tesla-9504443.

Black Oyibo. "Nji Collins Wins Google Code Award." YouTube video, 12:00. Posted March 2, 2017. https://www.youtube.com/watch?v=Taf2YFW4kjw. Accessed March 2017.

Bohn, Dieter. "Chasing the Next Billion with Sundar Pichai." Sundar's Google, *The Verge*, May 29, 2015. https://www.theverge.com/a/sundars-google/sundar-pichai-interview-google-io-2015.

Bohn, Dieter. "Slamdance: Inside the Weird Virtual Reality of Google's Project Tango." *The Verge*, May 29, 2015. https://www.theverge.com/a/sundars-google/project-tango-google-io-2015.

Bort, Julie. "Despite Setbacks and Job Cuts, Google Is Promising a Big Update in Its Race Against Amazon's Delivery Drones." *Business Insider*, April 29, 2017. http://www.businessinsider.com/a-closely-watched-google-x-project-cut-employees-2017-4.

Bort, Julie. "Twitter's Former Head Engineer Is Now Helping Larry Page Build Self-Flying Cars." *Business Insider*, March 7, 2017. http://www.businessinsider.com/alex-roetter-former-twitter-head-engineer-at-kitty-hawk-2017-3.

Boudette, Neal E. "G.M. Expands Self-Driving Car Operations in Silicon Valley." *New York Times*, April 13, 2017. https://www.nytimes.com/2017/04/13/business/gm-expands-self-driving-car-operations-to-silicon-valley.html.

Brandt, Richard L. *The Google Guys: Inside the Brilliant Minds of Google Founders Larry Page and Sergey Brin.* New York: Portfolio, 2011.

Brin, Sergey. "Remembering Rajeev." *Too* (blog). June 5, 2009. http://too.blogspot.com/2009/06/remembering-rajeev.html.

Brin, Sergey, and Larry Page. "The Genesis of Google." Filmed February 2004 at TED2004, Monterey, CA. TED video, 20:33. https://www.ted.com/talks/sergey_brin_and_larry_page_on_google.

Brin, Sergey, and Larry Page. "2014 Founders' IPO Letter." Alphabet Investor Relations. abc.xyz/investor/founders-letters/2004/ipo=letter.html.

Buchheit, Paul. "The Technology." *Paul Buchheit* (blog). July 30, 2014. http://paulbuchheit.blogspot.co.uk/2014/07/the-technology.html.

Burning Man. https://burningman.org.

Carlson, Nicholas. "The Untold Story of Larry Page's Incredible Comeback." *Business Insider*, April 24, 2014. http://www.businessinsider.com/larry-page-the-untold-story-2014-4.

CNBC. "Google's Sergey Brin Joins Anti-Travel Ban Protests at San Francisco Airport, Says 'I'm a Refugee.'" TECH: The Verge, January 29, 2017. http://www.cnbc.com/2017/01/29/googles-sergey-brin-joins-anti-travel-ban-protests-at-san-francisco-airport-says-im-a-refugee.html.

Diamandis, Peter H. and Marcus Shingles. "An Important Update from Google Lunar XPRIZE." *Google Lunar XPRIZE*. January 23, 2018. lunar.xprize.org/news/blog/important-update-google-lunar-xprize.

Dowd, Maureen. "Elon Musk's Billion-Dollar Crusade to Stop the A.I. Apocalypse." Hive, *Vanity Fair*, April 2017. http://www.vanityfair.com/news/2017/03/elon-musk-billion-dollar-crusade-to-stop-ai-space-x.

Drummond, David. "A New Approach to China: An Update." *Official Blog*. Google, March 22, 2010. https://googleblog.blogspot.com/2010/03/new-approach-to-china-update.html.

Edelhauser, Kristin. "Watching YouTube." *Entrepreneur*, October 12, 2006. https://www.entrepreneur.com/article/168764.

Elgan, Mike. "Google Glass Strikes Back." *Computerworld*, August 20, 2016. http://www.computerworld.com/article/3109502/wearables/google-glass-strikes-back.html.

Entrepreneur. "Larry Page and Sergey Brin." Growth Strategies, October 16, 2008. https://www.entrepreneur.com/article/197848.

Feynman, Richard P. *"Surely You're Joking, Mr. Feynman!": Adventures of a Curious Character.* London: W. W. Norton, 1985.

Feynman, Richard P. *"What Do You Care What Other People Think?": Further Adventures of a Curious Character.* London: W. W. Norton, 1988.

Forbes. "The Richest People in Tech: #5 Larry Page." Accessed August 3, 2017. https://www.forbes.com/profile/larry-page.

Forbes. "The Richest People in Tech: #6 Sergey Brin." Accessed August 3, 2017. https://www.forbes.com/profile/sergey-brin.

Fortune Magazine. "Larry Page Talks Alphabet, Warren Buffett and Project Loon at Fortune Global Forum 2015 | Fortune." November 2, 2015. YouTube video, 23:52. https://www.youtube.com/watch?v=blAOPCNCszM.

Friend, Tad. "Silicon Valley's Quest to Live Forever." *New Yorker*, April 3, 2017. http://www.newyorker.com/magazine/2017/04/03/silicon-valleys-quest-to-live-forever.

Garrett French. "Craig Silverstein 1: Intro + How Google Began. You Tube video, 9:17. Posted November 1, 2006. https://www.youtube.com/watch? QVkWmYUwhH8.

Gelles, David. "In Silicon Valley, Mergers Must Meet the Toothbrush Test." DealBook, *New York Times*, August 17, 2014. https://dealbook.nytimes.com/2014/08/17/in-silicon-valley-mergers-must-meet-the-toothbrush-test.

Gilbert, Sara. *Built for Success: The Story of Google.* Mankato, MN: Creative Education, 2009.

Goode, Lauren. "Alphabet's Health Division Made a Better Smartwatch than Google Could." *The Verge*, April 14, 2017. https://www.theverge.com/2017/4/14/15305694/alphabet-verily-health-tracking-smartwatch-study-watch.

Google. "Google Announces Calico, a New Company Focused on Health and Well-being." Google news release, September 18, 2013. http://googlepress.blogspot.com/2013/09/calico-announcement.html.

Google. "Google Books History." Google Books. Accessed February 1, 2017. https://www.google.com/googlebooks/about/history.html.

Google. "Google Checks Out Library Books." Google news release, December 14, 2004. http://googlepress.blogspot.com/2004/12/google-checks-out-library-books.html.

Google. "Google Code of Conduct." Alphabet Investor Relations, October 12, 2017. http://abc.xyz/investor/other/google-code-of-conduct.html.

Google. "Google Names Dr. Eric Schmidt Chief Executive Officer." Google news release, August 6, 2001. http://googlepress.blogspot.com/2001/08/google-names-dr-eric-schmidt-chief.html.

Google. "Google Receives $25 Million in Equity Funding." Google news release, June 7, 1999. http://googlepress.blogspot.com/1999/06/google-receives-25-million-in-equity.html.

Google. "Journey under the Earth's Surface in Street View." *The Keyword* (blog). March 15, 2017. https://blog.google/products/maps/journey-under-earths-surface-street-view.

Google. "Larry Page's University of Michigan Commencement Address." YouTube video, 16:28. May 4, 2009. https://www.youtube.com/watch?v=qFb2rvmrahc.

Google. "Our Story: From the Garage to the Googleplex." Accessed August 2, 2017. https://www.google.com/about/our-story.

Google. "The Evolution of Search." YouTube video, 6:20. November 27, 2011. https://www.youtube.com/watch?v=mTBShTwCnD4.

Greene, Diane. "As G Suite Gains Traction in the Enterprise, G Suite's Gmail and Consumer Gmail to More Closely Align." *The Keyword* (blog). Google, June 23, 2017. https://blog.google/products/gmail/g-suite-gains-traction-in-the-enterprise-g-suites-gmail-and-consumer-gmail-to-more-closely-align.

Guarino, Ben, and Kristine Guerra. "Anti-Semitic Jokes Cause YouTube, Disney to Distance Themselves from PewDiePie." Morning Mix, *Washington Post*, February 14, 2017. https://www.washingtonpost.com/news/morning-mix/wp/2017/02/14/pewdiepie-youtubes-most-popular-star-dropped-by-disney-over-anti-semitic-jokes.

Hamen, Susan E. *Google: The Company and Its Founders*. Edina, MN: ABDO Publishing / Essential Library, 2011.

Harris, Mark. "Revealed: Sergey Brin's Secret Plans to Build the World's Biggest Aircraft." *Guardian*, May 26, 2017. https://www.theguardian.com/media/2017/may/26/google-sergey-brin-building-largest-aircraft.

Heath, Thomas. "Space-Mining May Be Only a Decade Away. Really." *Washington Post*, April 28, 2017. https://www.washingtonpost.com/business/space-mining-may-be-only-a-decade-away-really/2017/04/28/df33b31a-29ee-11e7-a616-d7c8a68c1a66_story.html.

Helft, Miguel. "With YouTube, Student Hits Jackpot Again." *New York Times*, October 12, 2006. http://www.nytimes.com/2006/10/12/technology/12tube.html.

Immigrant Learning Center, The. "Immigrant Entrepreneur Hall of Fame: Sergey Brin." Accessed August 27, 2016. www.ilctr.org/entrepreneur-hof/sergey-brin/.

Isaacson, Walter. *The Innovators: How a Group of Hackers, Geniuses, and Geeks Created the Digital Revolution*. New York: Simon & Schuster, 2014.

Kasner, Edward, and James R. Newman. *Mathematics and the Imagination*. New York: Simon and Schuster, 1940.

Kettler, Sara. "The Google Chronicles: 7 Facts on Founders Larry Page & Sergey Brin." Biography.com, August 19, 2014. http://www.biography.com/news/google-founders-history-facts.

Kitty Hawk. "Introducing the Kitty Hawk Flyer." April 24, 2017. YouTube video, 2:21. https://www.youtube.com/watch?v=mMWh4W1C2PM.

Konstantinides, Anneta. "Nice Work If You Can Get It: The World's Highest Earning YouTube Stars Who Make up to $15m a Year from Their Online Shows." *Daily Mail*, December 6, 2016, updated December 7, 2016. http://www.dailymail.co.uk/news/article-4007938/The-10-Highest-Paid-YouTube-stars.html.

Lardinois, Frederic. "How Alphabet's Project Loon Balloons Learned to Loiter." TechCrunch.com, February 16, 2017. https://techcrunch.com/2017/02/16/how-googles-project-loon-balloons-learned-to-loiter.

Levy, Steven. *In the Plex: How Google Thinks, Works, and Shapes Our Lives*. New York: Simon & Schuster, 2011.

Lewis-Kraus, Gideon. "The Great A.I. Awakening." *New York Times Magazine*, December 14, 2016. https://www.nytimes.com/2016/12/14/magazine/the-great-ai-awakening.html.

Lohr, Steve. "Interview: Sergey Brin on Google's China Move." Bits, *New York Times*, March 22, 2010. https://bits.blogs.nytimes.com/2010/03/22/interview-sergey-brin-on-googles-china-gambit.

Mac, Ryan. "'Pokémon GO's' Creator Answers All Your Burning Questions (Except That One About Finding Pokémon)." *Forbes*, July 28, 2016. http://www.forbes.com/sites/ryanmac/2016/07/28/pokemon-go-creator-john-hanke-answers-all-your-burning-questions.

Mac, Ryan. "The Inside Story of 'Pokémon GO's' Evolution from Google Castoff to Global Phenomenon." *Forbes*, July 26, 2016. http://www.forbes.com/sites/ryanmac/2016/07/26/monster-game.

Malseed, Mark. "The Story of Sergey Brin." *Moment*, May 6, 2013. https://www.momentmag.com/the-story-of-sergey-brin. Previously published in Arts & Culture, *Moment*, February–March 2007.

Marcovitz, Hal. *Larry Page, Sergey Brin, and Google*. San Diego, CA: Reference Point, 2016.

Markoff, John. "No Longer a Dream: Silicon Valley Takes On the Flying Car." *New York Times*, April 24, 2017. https://www.nytimes.com/2017/04/24/technology/flying-car-technology.html.

Mathes, Adam. "The Point of Google Print." *Official Blog*. Google, October 19, 2005. https://googleblog.blogspot.com/2005/10/point-of-google-print.html. Includes editorial previously published as "Books of Revelation" by Eric Schmidt. *Wall Street Journal*, October 18, 2005.

Mattise, Nathan. "Project Loon Team Gave Puerto Rico Connectivity." *Ars Technica*, February 18, 2018. arstechnica.com/science/2018/02/project-loon-engineer-sees-a-tool-for-future-disaster-response-in-Puerto-Rico/.

McCracken, Harry. "How Gmail Happened: The Inside Story of Its Launch 10 Years Ago." *Time*, April 1, 2014. http://time.com/43263/gmail-10th-anniversary.

McCracken, Harry, and Lev Grossman. "Google vs. Death." *Time*, September 30, 2013. http://content.time.com/time/subscriber/article/0,33009,2152422,00.html.

McFarland, Matt. "Google Uses AI to Help Diagnose Breast Cancer." CNN Tech online, March 3, 2017. http://money.cnn.com/2017/03/03/technology/google-breast-cancer-ai.

McGregor, Jena. "Google Wants to Fix Tech's Diversity Problem with an Outpost for Historically Black Colleges." On Leadership, *Washington Post*, March 23, 2017. https://www.washingtonpost.com/news/on-leadership/wp/2017/03/23/google-wants-to-fix-techs-diversity-problem-with-an-outpost-for-historically-black-colleges.

McGuigan, Cathal. "Viral Video 'Alberto's Story' Puts Portadown on the Map." *Irish News*, November 27, 2015. http://www.irishnews.com/sport/footballsoccer/2015/11/27/news/viral-video-alberto-s-story-puts-portadown-on-the-map-336307.

Metz, Cade. "For Google, the AI Talent Race Leads Straight to Canada." *Wired*, March 30, 2017. https://www.wired.com/2017/03/google-ai-talent-race-leads-straight-canada.

MIT Technology Review. "Mobile Makeover." Graphiti, October 22, 2013. https://www.technologyreview.com/s/520491/mobile-makeover.

National Museum of American History, Smithsonian. "Google 'Corkboard' Server, 1999." Fact Sheets. http://americanhistory.si.edu/press/fact-sheets/google-corkboard-server-1999.

National Safety Council. "Motor Vehicle Deaths Increase by Largest Percent in 50 Years." National Safety Council news release, February 17, 2016. http://www.nsc.org/Connect/NSCNewsReleases/Lists/Posts/Post.aspx?ID=103.

Nieva, Richard. "Project Loon, Alphabet's Wi-Fi-Beaming Moon Shot, Still Flying." *CNET*, February 16, 2017. https://www.cnet.com/news/google-alphabet-project-loon-lab-astro-teller.

Olah, Chris. "Bringing Precision to the AI Safety Discussion." *Google Research Blog*. June 21, 2016. https://research.googleblog.com/2016/06/bringing-precision-to-ai-safety.html.

Page, Larry. "G Is for Google." *The Keyword* (blog). Google, August 10, 2015. https://blog.google/topics/alphabet/google-alphabet.

Page, Larry. Google + Post. July 18, 2013. https://plus.google.com/+LarryPage/posts/QVbFayWxfrm.

Page, Larry. "Where's Google Going Next?" Filmed March 2014 at TED2014, Vancouver, Canada. TED video, 23:30. https://www.ted.com/talks/larry_page_where_s_google_going_next.

PC Magazine Online. Via Internet Archive WayBack Machine. https://web.archive.org /web/19990508042436/www.zdnet.com/pcmag/special/web100/search2.html.

Perez, Juan Carlos, for IDG News Service. "Yahoo Increases E-Mail Capacity." *PCWorld*, June 15, 2004. http://www.pcworld.com/article/116514/article.html.

Portadown Times. "Portadown Teenager Alberto Balde Confirms Deal with Middlesbrough." Football, April 1, 2017. http://www.portadowntimes.co.uk/sport/football/portadown -teenager-alberto-balde-confirms-deal-with-middlesbrough-1-7896074.

Price, Rob, and Reuters. "The EU's Tough New Privacy Proposals Could Rip a Chunk out of Tech Companies' Ad Revenues." *Business Insider*, January 11, 2017. http://www.businessinsider .com/eu-privacy-proposals-ad-revenues-facebook-google-microsoft-others-2017-1.

Project Loon. "Balloon-Powered Internet for Everyone." Accessed March 20, 2017. https://x .company/loon.

Rainsford, Sarah. "How Russia's YouTube Generation Is Getting Its News." *BBC News* online, April 2, 2017. http://www.bbc.com/news/world-europe-39456232.

Reed, Sam. "Jennifer Lopez's Famous Grammys Dress Helped Spawn Google Images." Pret-a-Reporter, *The Hollywood Reporter*, April 8, 2015. http://www.hollywoodreporter.com/news /jennifer-lopezs-2000-grammys-dress-787251.

Regalado, Antonio. "Google's Long, Strange Life-Span Trip." Rewriting Life, *MIT Technology Review*, December 15, 2016. https://www.technologyreview.com/s/603087/googles-long -strange-life-span-trip.

Rohde, Laura, for IDG News Service. "Privacy Issues Plague Google's Gmail." *PCWorld*, April 15, 2004. http://www.pcworld.com/article/115692/article.html.

Ross, Alec. *Industries of the Future*. New York: Simon & Schuster, 2017.

Schmidt, Eric. "Books of Revelation." *Wall Street Journal*. October 18, 2005. https://www.wsj .com/articles/SB112958982689471238.

Schmidt, Eric, Jonathan Rosenberg, and Alan Eagle. *Google: How Google Works*. New York: Grand Central Publishing, 2014.

Schwartz, John. "Google Co-Founder Books a Space Flight." *New York Times*, June 11, 2008. http://www.nytimes.com/2008/06/11/technology/11soyuz.html.

Science Kids. "Nikola Tesla Facts." Last modified July 8, 2016. http://www.sciencekids.co.nz /sciencefacts/scientists/nikolatesla.html.

Smith, Dave. "Read Larry Page's New Letter about the Current Status of Alphabet, Google's Parent Company." Tech Insider, *Business Insider*, April 27, 2017. http://www.businessinsider .com/read-alphabet-ceo-larry-page-2016-letter-to-shareholders-2017-4.

Stanford University. "The Autism Glass Project at Stanford Medicine." Accessed April 2, 2017. http://autismglass.stanford.edu.

Stanford University. "The Original GOOGLE Computer Storage [Page and Brin] (1996)." Accessed August 22, 2016. http://infolab.stanford.edu/pub/voy/museum/pictures/display/0 -4-Google.htm.

Startup Cat. "Google Founders Interview—Larry Page and Sergey Brin." Interview by Vinod Khosla of Khosla Ventures. Filmed July 3, 2014, at KV CEO Summit. YouTube video, 41:55. Posted November 29, 2016. https://www.youtube.com/watch?v=GpjOZGxKhRM.

Stockton, Kara. "Make the Most of Father's Day with a Little Help from Your Assistant." *The Keyword* (blog). Google, June 16, 2017. https://blog.google/products/assistant/make-most -fathers-day-with-help-from-your-assistant.

Strom, Stephanie. "Billionaire Aids Charity that Aided Him." *New York Times*, October 24, 2009. http://www.nytimes.com/2009/10/25/us/25donate.html.

Stross, Randall E. *Planet Google: One Company's Audacious Plan to Organize Everything We Know*. New York: Free Press, 2008.

Sullivan, Danny. "Was It Time for a Fresh Face? Thoughts on Larry Page as the New Google CEO." Search Engine Land, January 20, 2011. http://searchengineland.com/googles-eric -schmidt-stepping-down-cofounder-larry-page-to-be-google-ceo-61883.

Swisher, Kara. "End of an Era: Google's Very First Employee, Craig Silverstein—Technically, No. 3—Leaving." *All Things D* (blog). February 9, 2012. http://allthingsd.com/20120209/googles-very-first-employee-craig-silverstein-technically-no-3-leaving.

Tsukayama, Hayley. "How Google and Levi's Smart Jacket Shows What's Coming Next for Wearables." *Washington Post*, March 14, 2017. https://www.washingtonpost.com/news/the-switch/wp/2017/03/14/how-google-and-levis-smart-jacket-shows-whats-coming-next-for-wearables.

Turovsky, Barak. "Fútbol, Translated." *The Keyword* (blog). Google, October 19, 2015. https://blog.google/products/translate/futbol-translated.

Turovsky, Barak. "Ten Years of Google Translate." *The Keyword* (blog). Google, April 28, 2016. https://www.blog.google/products/translate/ten-years-of-google-translate.

Ulanoff, Lance. "Is Gmail Safe?" *PC Magazine*, April 21, 2004. http://www.pcmag.com/article2/0,2817,1571462,00.asp.

Verily Life Sciences. "Liftware." Projects. Accessed June 21, 2017. https://verily.com/projects/interventions/liftware.

Verily Life Sciences. "Verily Launches Landmark Study with Duke and Stanford as First Initiative of Project Baseline." Project Baseline news release, *Business Wire*, April 19, 2017. http://www.businesswire.com/news/home/20170419005505/en/Verily-Launches-Landmark-Study-Duke-Stanford-Initiative.

Vise, David A., and Mark Malseed. *The Google Story.* New York: Delta, 2008.

Waddell, Kaveh. "Why Google Quit China—and Why It's Heading Back." *Atlantic*, January 19, 2016. https://www.theatlantic.com/technology/archive/2016/01/why-google-quit-china-and-why-its-heading-back/424482.

Wakabayashi, Daisuke. "Google Training Ad Placement Computers to Be Offended." *New York Times*, April 3, 2017. https://www.nytimes.com/2017/04/03/technology/google-training-ad-placement-computers-to-be-offended.html.

Waymo. "Say Hello to Waymo." December 13, 2016. YouTube video, 1:53. https://www.youtube.com/watch?v=uHbMt6WDhQ8. Features interview with first passenger of first fully self-driving car.

Whitwam, Ryan. "Niantic Made Almost $1 Billion in 2016, So Why Is Pokémon GO Still So Lame?" *Forbes*, January 19, 2017. http://www.forbes.com/sites/ryanwhitwam/2017/01/19/niantic-made-almost-1-billion-in-2016-so-why-is-pokemon-go-still-so-lame.

World Economic Forum. "Davos 2017—An Insight, an Idea with Sergey Brin." Filmed January 19, 2017 at annual meeting in Davos, Switzerland. YouTube video, 34:00. https://www.youtube.com/watch?v=ffvu6Mr1SVc.

ACKNOWLEDGMENTS

WHEN I STARTED THIS JOURNEY TO RESEARCH Google, an unexpected gift rose from the mountain of facts: the joy of studying the amazing contributions of immigrants, refugees, and big thinkers from around the world, from every walk of life and ability. What a treasure. To all the people who figure in to that story, I am grateful beyond words.

The opportunity to follow the trail blazed by Larry and Sergey has been moving, powerful, and fun. This book is the brainchild of my talented editor, Holly West. I am thankful that she trusted me with this incredible project. Thank you to Holly, Jean Feiwel, and the entire team at Feiwel and Friends for your support, hard work, and enthusiasm.

As powerful as today's technology is, there is still something magical about a librarian's ability to put the right book in your hand at the right moment. I owe a debt of gratitude to Super Librarian Kim Campbell and her amazing team (Molly and Jess) at the South Portland Public Library of South Portland, Maine.

Team Anna is large and their efforts overwhelming. My family and friends have had a front-row seat to this crazy publishing journey and have been a source of sunshine and strength every step of the way. Michael Redding has repeatedly stepped up to care for our boys so I can shoot for the moon. His support and encouragement are appreciated. My Cape Elizabeth Gang o' Moms are a constant source of optimism and laughs. And to my cheerleader-in-chief, my father, thank you.

I have two of the best brothers in the world: Patrick Crowley lent his expertise to this project, while Tim Crowley offered me a special gift: being proud of me.

A writer is lost without a critique group. My group has kept me from quitting at least three times. Thank you to Darlene Ivy, Helen Stevens, Laurie Warchol, Melanie Ellsworth, and Rebekah Lowell. My EMLA family is invaluable. I still pinch myself that I get to be a part of your clan.

And to the incomparable Ammi-Joan Paquette, my agent. You are a rock, a guiding hand, and a dear friend. Boy, am I lucky!

To all the Googlers (and Alphabeters) out there, your stories, your work, even your missteps will inspire readers you may never meet, and one day I bet they'll inspire you right back.

To readers everywhere, especially those of you who are finding your way through difficult circumstances or struggling to confront a tsunami of society-driven labels, this book is for you and all that you are truly capable of. Believe it.

● ● ○ ●

Anna Crowley Redding is the author of *Google It*, *Elon Musk: A Mission to Save the World*, and *Black Hole Chasers*. Her first career was as an Emmy award–winning investigative television reporter, anchor, and journalist. The recipient of multiple Edward R. Murrow awards and recognized by the Associated Press for her reporting, Crowley Redding now focuses her stealthy detective skills on digging up great stories for young readers. Anna's books have been recognized by NSTA as best STEM books.

annacrowleyredding.com